The best T E X - M E X combines the deep traditions of Texan and Mexican cooking, teasing out their nuances and highlighting their unique flavors, ingredients, and techniques. It is a cuisine built on deliciousness, textures—melty, crunchy, chewy—surprising flavor combinations, and the frontier spirit that motivated someone to make a piecrust out of Fritos.

T E X - M E X is the cuisine that chef Josef Centeno grew up with in San Antonio, Texas. It's the food that fuels the delicious, inventive, cross-cultural dishes he serves at his restaurants in Los Angeles. It's the casual, irresistible food he cooks with his family. And now it's the food you can cook at home, too.

Brimming with T E X - M E X dishes like you've never had them before, *Amá* takes on classics such as huevos rancheros, breakfast tacos, and enchiladas—along with one raging nacho party. Organized into chapters by type of food—breakfasts, salads, meats, drinks and desserts, and a tantalizing array of snacks and munchies, this beautifully photographed cookbook contains down-home cooking interwoven with the story of a deeply rooted T E X - M E X family and their love of food.

Bring the very best of what this marriage of cultures and flavors offers to your own table.

AMÁ

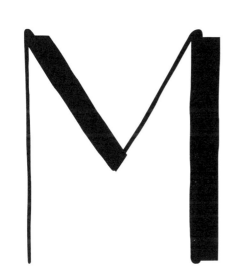
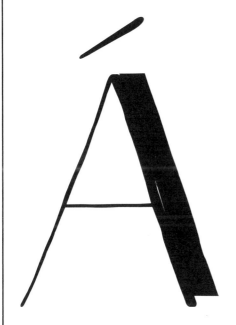

AMÁ

A MODERN TEX-MEX
KITCHEN

JOSEF CENTENO
&
BETTY HALLOCK

PHOTOGRAPHS BY
REN FULLER

CHRONICLE BOOKS
SAN FRANCISCO

Library of Congress Cataloging-in-Publication Data available.

ISBN 978-1-4521-5586-9

Manufactured in China.

MIX
Paper from
responsible sources
FSC
www.fsc.org
FSC™ C008047

Prop styling by ALICIA BUSZCZAK.
Food styling by JOSEF CENTENO.
Design by VANESSA DINA.
Typesetting by FRANK BRAYTON.

10 9 8 7 6 5 4 3 2 1

Chronicle books and gifts are available at special quantity discounts to corporations, professional associations, literacy programs, and other organizations. For details and discount information, please contact our premiums department at corporatesales@chroniclebooks.com or at 1-800-759-0190.

Chronicle Books LLC
680 Second Street
San Francisco, California 94107
WWW.CHRONICLEBOOKS.COM

INTRODUCTION

Bar Amá isn't so much a bar as it is a neighborhood restaurant—a small, noisy, friendly Tex-Mex joint, not in Texas but in the center of downtown Los Angeles, next to an alley off of Fourth Street. Why Tex-Mex? I don't know if anyone would call it a trending cuisine. In fact, some say the opposite. I'd turned my back on it once, too.

Born and raised in San Antonio, I was a fairly normal angsty kid who loved skateboarding and punk music and rejected almost everything else. I wanted to escape from Catholic school, private military academy, cotillion classes, even summer trips to the Gulf Coast—all the things my parents worked so hard to give me (I'm sorry for being an ingrate, Mom and Dad). I wanted to be a chef, left for New York, and never looked back at the queso.

Until one day I did. I had cooked for Michelin three-star chefs at restaurants in New York, San Francisco, and Santa Cruz—French haute cuisine, Japanese-influenced omakase, progressive Spanish tasting menus. When I opened my own first restaurant in Los Angeles, Bäco Mercat, I tapped into a sort of reimagined cuisine heavily influenced by the cooking of the Mediterranean—Spanish, Italian, Portuguese, Moroccan, and Lebanese flavors, with a little Ethiopian and Asian, too.

But there was a kernel of a memory that was Tex-Mex. Maybe it had something to do with all the breakfast tacos and enchiladas and fajitas I loved to eat. So I went back to San Antonio, and I ate at all the old-school spots. But the tacos and queso and margaritas weren't all that I was looking for. I realized there was another Tex-Mex, one that was connected to four generations of Tejanos on both sides of my family.

Joe Centeno Sr., my great-grandfather, had nothing when he arrived in San Antonio from northern Mexico, a doctor's son who wanted to go his own way. But he and my great-grandmother eventually founded the first independent chain of Latino supermarkets in Texas. Before my family lost it all (the other side of the great American success story), I spent holidays at the ranch that Joe Sr. built. For big family get-togethers, there would be barbacoa and cabrito, *borracho* beans, my great-grandmother's potato salad, and her homemade hot sauces.

On my mom's side, my great-grandparents barely escaped the Mexican Revolution alive. They settled and stayed in San Antonio's West Side neighborhood. There, everything revolved around my great-grandmother's tiny kitchen. She was the legendary cook in my family, known for making a delicious meal from only a few ingredients. She was Amá.

I finally realized that I wanted to honor the food I grew up with: fideo and tomatoes with cilantro and pork belly simmering on the stove, spicy menudo every Christmas and New Year's, egg salad between butter-toasted bolillos, and Tía Carmen's flour tortillas filled with *lengua* carnitas and crushed avocado, and doused with pequín chile salsa. These are some of the dishes that have inspired me—the food that I was nurtured with by the people who raised me. Named for my great-grandmother, Bar Amá is my version of their Tex-Mex.

THE LIFE AND TIMES OF
GABINA CERVANTES MARTINEZ

It's a miracle that my great-grandmother, Gabina Cervantes Martinez, ever made it to San Antonio and lived to be nearly ninety years old. I always knew her as Amá. That's what everyone called her, and to us it basically meant "boss lady." When I was growing up, she was my family's supreme matriarch, a living legend.

Amá met Eulojio Martinez, my Apá, in their hometown of Irapuato in the central state of Guanajuato, Mexico, in 1910. Eulojio already had been drafted to fight for federal forces in the Mexican Revolution, leaving behind his family's bakery, butcher shop, and café. They married in 1913. Amá was barely a teenager, but her father—once mayor of the town—and mother figured it would be safer for their daughter to be married than to stay at home, at a time when kidnappings and worse weren't uncommon. Apá was only a few years older.

Amá followed him as one of the war's legions of *soldaderas*, women who fought and camped with the army. For the most part, she managed to stick with Apá, even when he was captured. This happened so many times during the war that later he often joked about whose side he fought on. If a soldier was asked at gunpoint, "*Viva quien?*" ("Long live who?") and answered incorrectly, he was shot. Better to switch allegiances in a revolution that he felt had devolved into lawlessness than to be executed on the spot.

One of my uncles told me that at the Battle of Torréon, Apá had a cup of hot chocolate shot out of his hand. As a kid, that image stuck with me—it was like a scene from a cowboy movie. I guess that made it somehow relatable to a six-year-old who only knew the drag of chores and Catholic school and the bliss of watching cartoons. What did I understand of war and heartache?

In the middle of the war, Amá and Apá were traveling by rail across Mexico when their train rode over a bomb hidden beneath the tracks. (Soldiers were transported by boxcar, and women often rode separately, sometimes on top of the train—crazy.) The bomb detonated, and the train, which split in two, was attacked by enemy forces. In the chaos my great-grandparents were separated, and each feared that the other had been killed. Neither knew that the other had survived. Amá fled, and to make a living, she and her mother-in-law ended up making tacos and selling them to passengers at a train station in central Mexico.

Nearly two years later, Amá and Apá were reunited when she spotted him on the train platform. Fate! I think by then they already knew they had to leave Mexico. My mom, aunt, and uncles said Amá and Apá had always wanted to return to Guanajuato, but there wasn't much left for them there. Nearly two million people died during the war, and hundreds of thousands were displaced. So Amá and her mother-in-law waited in Nuevo Laredo, Mexico, near the U.S. border while Apá went to find work in the United States, first in Chicago and later in San Antonio.

As they had earlier in the war, Amá and her mother-in-law made and sold tacos and taquitos from a table at the train station. Amá figured that would be their reunion spot again—she would meet Apá there when he returned. After five years of separation and hardship (Amá never talked much about those years), including losing a daughter to whooping cough, they finally reached San Antonio together sometime around 1920. They settled in the West Side community that was home to others who had fled. This is where the story of my family in Texas starts, in the same neighborhood—a Mexican-American enclave since the 1700s—where San Antonio's Tex-Mex cuisine emerged.

AMÁ'S WEST SIDE KITCHEN

The West Side is the barrio where Amá's children—including my grandmother, Maria de la Luz Martinez (aka Nana)—grew up, a neighborhood of small family homes, bakeries, cafés, produce warehouses, packing plants, stockyards, and railroad depots.

Amá and Apá lived in a little aqua-trimmed house on Hazel Street, five blocks from the big produce market where truckloads of fruit and vegetables would arrive every morning for delivery to the city's grocery stores. I mostly remember Amá in the kitchen. Sometimes she and Apá would watch *lucha libre* (wrestling) or *telenovelas* (soaps) on TV or sit on their plant-covered porch watching the world (the two also occasionally attended bullfights in Nuevo Laredo). But Amá was always certain that the minute visitors arrived, they were hungry. So we'd end up in the kitchen at her little Formica table with green vinyl–covered chairs.

Her stove was a two-burner-plus-a-plancha, and I don't think the refrigerator was much bigger than a school locker. But it was like that small car with the implausible number of clowns—continuously full of fresh produce. Out would come corn, poblano chiles, yellow onions. This was partly because Apá owned and operated a vegetable stand at El Mercado, an outdoor plaza of shops and farmers' market stalls built as a Works Progress Administration project in downtown San Antonio. My mom said she would visit when she was a tiny kid and sit on the scales.

Something was usually bubbling on Amá's stove, refried beans or the start of her fideo. She didn't particularly like spicy stuff, but Apá did. So she would pick pequín chiles, which they grew in their backyard; drop them into a *molcajete* (mortar) with some salt; and grind a rustic salsa.

Amá's kitchen was a tiny theater for a kind of magic show, where with a few ingredients and a modest flurry, there would be this ta-da moment when she passed you a freshly rolled enchilada—just a little bit of cheese inside a tortilla she'd warmed in hot oil and topped with her sofrito, which was finely diced carrots and potatoes and a little bit of onion. She made tomato consommé and fideo, rolled her own tortillas, prepared her own salsas, and cooked with a lot of fresh vegetables—from the farmers' market or her own yard.

This is the version of Tejano cooking that I grew up with—simple cooking that wasn't authentically Mexican but not the melted-cheese-topped stuff people usually talk about when describing Tex-Mex. I have a photo of Amá in her seventies, standing by a stove of course, wearing a simple dress and an apron, because she was always wearing an apron. She was stocky, with white hair, glasses, and leathery skin. She looks both nurturing and formidable at the same time. That photo hangs in the kitchen at Bar Amá, a reminder of what Tex-Mex means to me.

TEX-MEX IN LOS ANGELES

Traditional Tex-Mex is rancho food—grilled or braised meats, stews, beans, chiles, and tortillas, especially flour tortillas (in my family, anyway). Beyond the queso and chili gravy, you might make out the rough outline of Mexico's Norteño cuisine (especially the meats and flour tortillas). I grew up on a lot of what the rest of America ate, but also family dishes such as carne guisada, chiles rellenos, picadillo, *calabacitas*, migas, and fajitas. Also Ms. Miller's BBQ, Luby's Cafeteria for biscuits and gravy, and the original Cristian's Tacos (RIP) for breakfast tacos. The Tex-Mex I love is soulful, fresh food.

Tex-Mex was largely dismissed by the culinary elite in the 1970s as inauthentic Mexican food. But that's the point. The only thing authentic about Tex-Mex is that it isn't authentic: It evolves and adapts. And Bar Áma is as much an L.A. restaurant as it is anything else. What's on the menu revolves around produce from farmers' markets and local meat and seafood, and a lot of the dishes might not be considered traditional Tex-Mex: escarole with watermelon radishes (page 117), slow-roasted beef belly (page 89), whole sea bream with cilantro chimichurri (page 107). But it is.

Part of the Bar Amá menu reflects Tex-Mex the way I remember it and family traditions that might otherwise have been lost. And hopefully we're reclaiming the nachos and queso and margaritas of popular Tex-Mex from the cheapened versions proliferated by corporate chains. We make everything from scratch. All of the tortillas are made by hand at the restaurant. We source non-GMO masa. Our eggs come from a friend's free-range chickens. We use heritage-breed pork and sustainably raised beef. It's like the Tex-Mex of my West Side family before anybody called anything either Tex-Mex or organic.

Tex-Mex is diverse—with influences from the American South, Germany, Poland, and Morocco (thanks to immigrants by way of the Canary Islands). Our kitchen finds inspiration from regional Mexican cuisine and beyond. And because we're in Los Angeles, we use a lot of local fruits and vegetables—broccolini, cauliflower, escarole, corn, heirloom tomatoes, stone fruit, gooseberries, sweet potatoes, jicama, squash blossoms. We even serve vegan queso.

There are some Tex-Mex dishes that I want to preserve because they're comfort foods. But there is room for a new kind of Tex-Mex that continues to evolve and can thrive beyond Texas, beyond Los Angeles—anywhere.

A NOTE ON CHILES: I use a lot of them, fresh and dried. Often the fresh and dried versions of the same chile go by different names. An ancho chile, for example, is a dried poblano. But some chiles that are used fresh or dried go by the same name—for example, arbol and New Mexico chiles. In that case, I make it clear in the ingredients list which type you need.

BIG S
PRODUCE

LARD

R

Preserved lemons are common in Middle Eastern cuisine, but I've played with preserving various kinds of citrus. I tried limes, but they always come out super bitter. Bergamot and Seville oranges are better for marmalades. I really like kumquats here: They're tart, but the peel is sweet, and the whole fruit—pith, peel, and all—is edible. Lime juice boosts the acidity, and grating in the zest of the limes adds another layer of citrus flavor.

NOTE: Oregano Indio is available online from Rancho Gordo.

MAKES 1 PT (230 G)

14 to 18 kumquats (enough to fit in a 1 pt [480 ml] jar), rinsed

1 or 2 dried arbol chiles, stemmed and seeded

¼ cup [75 g] fine sea salt

1 tsp dried Mexican oregano, preferably Oregano Indio

½ cup [120 ml] fresh lime juice

⅛ tsp grated lime zest

Put a 1 pt [480 ml] canning jar and lid in a large pot and cover with water. Bring to a boil over high heat. Carefully remove the jar and lid with tongs and let dry on a clean towel or rack.

Toast the arbol chiles in a small, dry skillet over medium heat to release the oils, shaking the pan occasionally to prevent the chiles from burning, about 1 minute. Set aside.

Cut each kumquat in half from top to bottom, stopping about ½ in [12 mm] from the base, so that it is still intact. Mix the salt with the oregano. Tear the toasted chiles into the salt mixture (you can leave the pieces fairly large). With clean hands, put about ½ tsp of the salt mixture into a kumquat and squeeze over the prepared jar to release the juices while retaining the salt mixture. Put the kumquat in the jar. Repeat with the remaining kumquats.

Pour any remaining salt mixture over the kumquats in the jar. Add the lime juice and zest; the kumquats should be submerged. Cover with the lid and seal. Gently shake to help the salt dissolve.

Leave the jar in a cool spot in the kitchen for 10 days, gently shaking the jar every day or so. Rinse the kumquats before using or use straight from the jar. They will keep, covered, in the refrigerator for up to 2 months.

17

Preserved kumquats, salty and tart-sweet, make a great vinaigrette. I like the combination of kumquats, shallots, and serrano chiles here. Use this dressing for just about any salad.

MAKES ABOUT ½ CUP (120 ML)

4 preserved kumquats with lime and chile (page 17), finely chopped

2 small shallots, finely chopped

12 thin slices serrano chile (or adjust to desired spiciness)

Juice of 2 lemons

Juice of 2 limes

¼ cup [60 ml] extra-virgin olive oil

Fresh black pepper

Mix the kumquats, shallots, and chiles in a small bowl. Whisk in the lemon juice, lime juice, and olive oil. Add several grinds of black pepper and whisk to combine. Serve immediately or store in a covered container in the refrigerator for up to 1 week.

This is one of my favorite dressings, based on the flavors of "Italian dressing"—olive oil and lots of garlic—but made with hoja santa, "or holy leaf." Hoja santa is an herb with big, floppy leaves that tastes slightly of anise, tarragon, sassafras, and mint. At Bar Amá we use it in chile pastes, salsas, soups, and beans. I've also used it to wrap vegetables before roasting and added it to infusions for ice cream. Sometimes I toast it a little over an open flame to bring out the oils before adding it to a recipe. It's definitely a favorite herb. We're lucky to get it fresh here in Los Angeles; I grow a big pot of it at home.

NOTE : Fresh hoja santa is available at Latino markets. You can substitute dried hoja santa, also available at Latino markets and online. One caveat: Dried hoja santa should have a pleasant, subtle anise flavor. If it doesn't, it's been on the shelf too long.

MAKES ABOUT ½ CUP (120 ML)

1 small fresh hoja santa leaf (or ½ large leaf), or 1 tsp dried hoja santa

1 garlic clove, grated with a rasp-style grater

2 Tbsp fresh yuzu juice, or juice of 1 lime

¼ tsp fresh black pepper

Pinch of fine sea salt

⅓ cup [80 ml] extra-virgin olive oil

Pass the fresh hoja santa leaf back and forth over the open flame of a gas burner so that it gets toasty and releases its oils, about 20 seconds. (You can use tongs for this.)

Finely chop the hoja santa and put it into a small jar with a lid. Add the garlic, yuzu juice, black pepper, and sea salt. Seal the jar, and shake to combine. Add the olive oil, reseal, and shake. Use immediately or store, covered, in the refrigerator for up to 1 week.

OREGANO VINAIGRETTE

Substitute 2 heaping tsp of dried Mexican oregano, preferably Oregano Indio (see Note, page 17), for the hoja santa.

A cascabel chile is a woody, acidic, slightly smoky dried chile, with nutty undertones. It isn't very hot, so it's great when you want to feature a chile flavor without too much spice. I like the combination of chiles and citrus, and the addition of herbaceous thyme—slightly lemony and slightly minty—too. It comes together as a zesty, spicy, savory dressing, which is great on salads or sliced jicama, papaya, or avocado.

MAKES ABOUT ½ CUP (120 ML)

2 cascabel chiles, stemmed and seeded

1 Tbsp fresh thyme leaves

1 garlic clove, grated with a rasp-style grater

3 Tbsp fresh lime juice

Fresh black pepper

Pinch of fine sea salt

⅓ cup [80 ml] avocado oil

Tear the chiles into large pieces. Toast in a small, dry skillet until they begin to soften and change color, 1 to 2 minutes. Cool, and then crumble the chiles.

Put the chiles in a small jar with a lid. Add the thyme leaves, garlic, lime juice, 3 or 4 grinds of black pepper, and sea salt. Seal the jar and shake to combine. Add the avocado oil, reseal, and shake. Use immediately or store, covered, in the refrigerator for up to 1 week.

I've eaten more canned carrot escabeche than I care to remember. Sure, I liked those sliced carrots—and jalapeños and onions—from cans. But now that I live in Southern California and have access to fresh vegetables year-round, I can pickle vegetables and chiles straight from the farmers' market. I like using small, whole carrots. They take the vinegar and chile flavor well, and they keep a lot of their crunch.

SERVES 4

8 baby carrots, peeled

5 cipollini or pearl onions

3 jalapeño chiles, stemmed, seeded, and sliced

4 garlic cloves, thinly sliced

2 sprigs fresh oregano, or 1 tsp dried Mexican oregano, preferably Oregano Indio (see Note, page 17)

¾ cup [180 ml] distilled white vinegar

¾ cup [180 ml] water

2 Tbsp sugar

Pinch of fine sea salt

Put the carrots, onions, jalapeños, garlic, and oregano in a medium heat-proof bowl or container.

Combine the vinegar, water, sugar, and salt in a small saucepan and bring to a boil. Pour the pickling liquid over the vegetables (the vegetables should be completely submerged in the pickling liquid). Cool to room temperature. Cover and refrigerate for at least 4 hours (overnight is best) before serving. Store, covered, in the refrigerator for up to 2 weeks.

At Bar Amá, we'll add a little habanero pickle to a salsa for an extra pop of flavor and heat. You can use it to garnish roasted fish, tacos, nachos, and ceviche. Or put a sliver on a nacho chip—one sliver goes a long way.

MAKES 3 CUPS (550 G)

8 oz [225 g] habanero chiles, stemmed

¼ tsp fennel seeds

¼ tsp ground coriander

¼ tsp dried Mexican oregano, preferably Oregano Indio (see Note, page 17)

1 small fresh bay leaf, or 2 dried

½ cup [120 ml] distilled white vinegar

½ cup [120 ml] water

½ cup [100 g] sugar

Wearing gloves, cut the habanero into thin slices, removing the seeds. Transfer to a large heat-proof bowl or container and set aside.

Toast the fennel seeds, coriander, oregano, and bay leaf in a small, dry skillet over medium heat, stirring frequently, until fragrant, 1 to 2 minutes. Remove from the heat.

Put the spices, vinegar, water, and sugar in a small saucepan and bring to a boil. Remove from the heat. Strain the liquid over the bowl of habanero slices, discarding the solids. Cool to room temperature. You can use this immediately, but it's better to let it sit in the refrigerator for at least 1 hour. Store in a covered container in the refrigerator for up to 2 weeks.

I like pickled onions with just about anything. Sharp, spicy, crunchy, and sour, they're both condiment and flavor enhancer. They taste especially great with barbecue because they help cut the richness of the meat. Put them on tacos, enchiladas, or piles of nachos. They're also great as a garnish for other vegetables and salads.

MAKES ABOUT 4 CUPS (885 G)

2 medium onions, cut into ¼ in [6 mm] rings

2 or 3 dried arbol chiles, stemmed and seeded

1½ cups [360 ml] distilled white vinegar

1½ cups [360 ml] water

2 tsp fine sea salt

2 tsp sugar

1½ Tbsp dried Mexican oregano, preferably Oregano Indio (see Note, page 17)

Put the onions in a medium heat-proof bowl or container.

Toast the chiles in a small, dry skillet over medium-high heat, stirring constantly, until darkened and fragrant, 1 to 1½ minutes. Set aside.

Combine the vinegar, water, salt, and sugar in a medium saucepan and bring to a boil. Add the oregano and chiles and remove from the heat.

Pour the vinegar mixture over the onions (the onions should be completely submerged). Cool to room temperature. Refrigerate for 2 to 3 hours before using. Store, covered, for up to 2 weeks.

PICKLED OKRA

Replace the onions with 10 medium pods (about 3½ oz [100 g]) of okra, stemmed and halved lengthwise. Bring a pot of salted water to boil. Add the okra and blanch until just tender, 2 to 3 minutes. Drain immediately, and proceed with the recipe, pouring the pickling liquid over the okra. Store, covered, in the refrigerator for up to 3 days.

Found at farmers' markets and in sunny backyards, Cape gooseberries have a sweet-tart flavor, which tastes like a combination of cherry tomato, pineapple, mango, and Meyer lemon. Like tomatillos, they have a husk you have to remove before using. They're a good match with pickling spices—here, a little coriander, star anise, allspice, and pepper. And the pickling process really works its magic on the gooseberries, rounding out their tartness. Add these as a puckery condiment to salads, ceviches, and roasted and grilled meats—anything that could use a little fruity acidity.

MAKES ABOUT 4 CUPS (750 G)

¼ tsp coriander seeds

3 whole allspice

1 star anise

1 tsp black peppercorns

⅓ cup [80 ml] Champagne vinegar

⅓ cup [80 ml] water

⅓ cup [65 g] sugar

A few fresh cilantro leaves

Pinch of fine sea salt

2 cups [250 g] gooseberries, husked and halved

In a small, dry skillet, toast the coriander, allspice, star anise, and black peppercorns over medium heat, stirring frequently, until they begin to release their oils and are fragrant, about 2 minutes. Set aside.

Combine the vinegar, water, and sugar in a saucepan and bring to a boil. Remove from the heat, add the spices, and set the mixture aside to cool to room temperature.

Put the halved gooseberries in a container. When the vinegar mixture is cool, pour it over the gooseberries. Cover and refrigerate for at least 1 hour before using. Store, covered, in the refrigerator for up to 1 week.

This is a pico de gallo–style salsa, usually made with raw tomatoes. We call it salmorejo because it's inspired by the Spanish dish of puréed tomatoes. At Bar Amá, instead of chopped tomatoes, we grate fresh Roma tomatoes . . . until it isn't tomato season anymore. Then we turn to canned San Marzano tomatoes (which also can work well year-round). We use our own homemade chile powder mix, but you can use store-bought chile powder, such as Rancho Gordo, available online; add a little at a time if you want to adjust the heat level.

MAKES ABOUT 2 CUPS (480 ML)

½ small onion

1 garlic clove

5 large Roma tomatoes or whole canned San Marzano tomatoes

¼ cup [4 g] fresh cilantro leaves

½ chipotle chile in adobo

2 tsp Amá spice mix (page 32) or chile powder

1 tsp dried Mexican oregano, preferably Oregano Indio (see Note, page 17)

½ tsp fine sea salt

Fresh black pepper

Heat the broiler. Put the onion and garlic on a small baking sheet and broil until well browned, about 3 minutes. Flip them over and broil until the other side is browned, about 3 minutes. Remove from the oven and set aside.

Coarsely chop the tomatoes and put them in a food processor. Add the onion, garlic, cilantro, chipotle, spice mix, oregano, salt, and a few grinds of black pepper. Pulse until coarsely puréed. Adjust the salt to taste. Use immediately or store in a covered container in the refrigerator for up to 3 days.

This is one of the essential sauces at Bar Amá. We put it on chile shrimp fajitas (page 165) and on broccolini torrada with aged cheddar and lime (page 125). It also goes on salads, other vegetables, sautés, and ceviches, and into other sauces. During my snack breaks, I eat grilled chicken in a flour tortilla with Mexican sriracha pretty much daily. A little goes a long way because it's really spicy.

MAKES ABOUT 1½ CUPS (360 ML)

1 ½ Tbsp olive oil

1 ½ cups [45 g] dried arbol chiles

1 cup [160 g] sliced shallots (from about 6 shallots)

½ cup [120 ml] tomato sauce, or ½ cup [170 g] crushed San Marzano tomatoes

3 Tbsp sugar

7 garlic cloves, peeled

½ cup [120 ml] fish sauce, preferably Three Crabs or Red Boat

Scant ½ cup [100 ml] distilled white vinegar

½ cup [120 ml] water, or as needed

Heat the oil in a large skillet over medium-high heat until hot and shimmering. Add the chiles, shallots, tomato sauce, sugar, and garlic. Turn the heat to high and cook, stirring often, until the chiles and shallots soften, about 6 minutes. Remove from the heat and set aside to cool.

Put the chile mixture, fish sauce, and vinegar in a blender and blend on high speed, adding the water 1 Tbsp at a time, until liquefied and the consistency of a smooth sauce, about 5 minutes. Taste and add more fish sauce if desired.

Strain the mixture through a fine-mesh sieve set over a bowl and transfer to a jar with a lid. Discard the solids. Store, covered, in the refrigerator for up to 2 weeks.

This is the salsa that comes with every order of tortilla chips at Bar Amá. It's inspired by a recipe from chef de cuisine Francisco Flores's grand-mother, Josefina Gomez. Francisco says she usually uses a mixture of arbol and guajillo for her barbacoa and birria, but he's a huge fan of the smok-iness of chipotle. So we use morita chiles (morita is a common variety of chipotle chile, which is itself a smoked jalapeño). They're a good match with mild, bittersweet guajillo chiles—very balanced. The spice level, color, and the acidity are similar to Josefina's salsa. This is nice and salty, so it's great with margaritas. All in all, really addictive.

MAKES ABOUT 2 CUPS (480 ML)

3 morita chiles (or any variety of chipotle chile)

4 guajillo chiles

6 Roma tomatoes or whole canned San Marzano tomatoes

1½ tsp olive oil

1 Tbsp grated onion (use the largest holes of a box grater)

2 tsp fine sea salt

⅓ cup [80 ml] water

1 Tbsp distilled white vinegar

1½ Tbsp chopped fresh cilantro leaves

Heat the oven to 350°F [180°C].

Put the chiles on a baking sheet. Toast in the oven until fragrant and brittle, 6 to 8 minutes. Remove from the oven, transfer to a medium bowl, and set aside.

Position a rack about 4 in [10 cm] from the heat and turn on the broiler. Put the tomatoes on the baking sheet, and drizzle with the olive oil. Broil them until charred, 4 to 5 minutes. Flip the tomatoes and broil the other side, 4 to 5 minutes more. Remove from the oven and set aside to cool.

Put the chiles, tomatoes, onion, salt, water, vinegar, and cilantro in a blender and purée until smooth. Taste and adjust the salt and vinegar as desired. Store in a covered container in the refrigerator for up to 2 weeks.

As a kid, when I walked through our family's Centeno Super Market, I'd go straight to the chiles section. There was always a table displaying mounds of dried chiles of all kinds. It was a really fragrant experience—the caramel-y, leathery, tobacco-ish, spicy, fruity smell of chiles. As an adult, I have always been disappointed by commercial bottles of chili powder, which contain herbs and spices, as well as chiles, and don't taste or smell like chiles at all. So at Amá we always make our own with several kinds of dried chiles. It isn't exactly the same recipe every time. The flavors and heat levels of chiles change from season to season. They have their own terroir, and we kind of roll with it, changing the varieties and proportions with each batch. Once you start playing around with different chiles, you can make your own tweaks.

NOTE : The chiles in this recipe are all dried. When using chile powders and hot sauces, watch out for porous surfaces and dishes, which may stain. Wear gloves when handling a lot of chiles.

MAKES ABOUT 1½ CUPS (115 G)

8 dried arbol chiles

5 guajillo chiles

5 dried New Mexico chiles

5 chipotle chiles

4 chiles negro

4 mulato chiles

4 pasilla de Oaxaca chiles

4 cascabel chiles

1 tsp fine sea salt

Heat the oven to 350°F [180°C].

Put the chiles on a baking sheet and toast in the oven until fragrant and brittle, about 10 minutes. Set aside to cool.

Remove and discard the stems and seeds from the chiles. Tear the chiles into large pieces, grind to a fine powder in a spice grinder, and mix with the salt. Store in an airtight container or sealed plastic bag at room temperature for up to 1 month or in the freezer for up to 1 year.

This is a really easy hot sauce to make if you have chile powder on hand. I think of this as the make-anywhere hot sauce, because as long as you have chile powder, basically you just add distilled white vinegar, boil, and strain. You can adjust the sugar and salt to your liking, depending on the chiles in your mix.

MAKES 1½ CUPS (360 ML)

1 cup [240 ml] distilled white vinegar

¼ cup [60 ml] water

¼ cup plus 1 Tbsp [55 g] Amá spice mix (page 32)

2 garlic cloves, grated with a rasp-style grater, or 2 tsp garlic powder

2 Tbsp finely grated onion, or 2 tsp onion powder

2 tsp fine sea salt

1 tsp sugar

Combine all the ingredients in a small saucepan. Bring to a boil, and let boil for 1 minute. Remove from the heat. Carefully strain through a fine-mesh sieve set over small bowl. Store, covered, in a jar or bottle in the refrigerator for up to 2 months.

My great-grandmother Jesusita Centeno—or Mama Grande—loved salsas and hot sauces. From mild and sweet to hot, hot, hot. She loved all chiles. Her greatest disappointment when she visited Europe with my great-grandfather in the '50s was that she couldn't find chiles. When she finally found some at a small farmers' market in Paris, she bought the stand out, carrying them with her on the rest of the trip to add to her food. Her daughter, my grandmother, inherited her recipe for pequín salsa. Because she had a pequín bush, she made it with fresh chiles. Dried pequín are easier to source, though. This recipe doesn't make a lot, but it's just right for preparing with a mortar and pestle. It isn't too hot, and it's mildly sweet from the onions. It's great on everything.

MAKES ¾ CUP (180 ML)

8 fresh or dried pequín chiles
1 small tomato, coarsely chopped
1 tomatillo, husked, rinsed, and coarsely chopped
¼ white onion, coarsely chopped
1 garlic clove
2 Tbsp olive oil
½ tsp fine sea salt

If using dried pequín chiles, rehydrate them by pouring boiling water over them in a heat-proof bowl. Let sit for 5 minutes, and then drain.

Crush the chiles, tomato, tomatillo, onion, and garlic in a mortar and pestle until puréed.

Heat the olive oil in a small skillet over medium-high heat. Add the chile mixture and cook, stirring frequently, just until it reaches a boil, about 1 minute. Remove from the heat. Add the salt. Serve hot or at room temperature. Store, covered, in the refrigerator, for up to 2 days.

I use this coffee-and-chile spice mix as a rub for roasted or grilled chicken, lamb, and beef, as well as a seasoning for gravies and sauces. For a big punch of complex flavor, I love the combination of coffee with chile, cardamom, cumin, and other warm spices.

MAKES ABOUT ¾ CUP (70 G)

3 Tbsp finely ground coffee

2 Tbsp chipotle chile powder

2 Tbsp packed dark brown sugar

2 Tbsp dry mustard powder

1 Tbsp sweet paprika

2 tsp fresh black pepper

2 tsp dried Mexican oregano, preferably Oregano Indio (see Note, page 17)

½ tsp ground cumin

½ tsp ground caraway

½ tsp ground cardamom

½ tsp ground coriander

½ tsp ground cloves

½ tsp ground ginger

½ tsp ground turmeric

½ tsp ground cinnamon

½ tsp fine sea salt

Whisk together all the ingredients in a small bowl until well combined. Store at room temperature in a covered container for up to 1 month.

I grew up on guacamole. When we went to my great-grandfather's farm south of San Antonio for big family gatherings, there was always *aguacate* salsa. It wasn't quite guacamole, and it wasn't a classic taco truck avocado sauce, which is smooth and spicy. It had plenty of tomatillos and their tang.

NOTE : You don't have to roast the jalapeños; you can use them raw for their fresh, sharp flavor.

MAKES ABOUT 1 CUP (240 ML)

6 oz [170 g] tomatillos, husked and rinsed

Fine sea salt

2 medium jalapeño chiles

¼ ripe avocado

¼ cup [7 g] chopped fresh cilantro leaves

2 Tbsp distilled white vinegar or rice vinegar

Heat the broiler.

Put the tomatillos on a foil-lined baking sheet and sprinkle with a pinch of salt. Broil until charred and softened, 3 to 5 minutes, flipping over with tongs halfway through cooking. Remove from the oven and cool slightly.

Using tongs (or skewering the chiles), roast the jalapeños over the open flame of a gas burner, turning the chiles until blackened on all sides, 1 to 2 minutes. Transfer to a small bowl and cover with plastic wrap. Set aside to steam for 10 minutes.

Once the chiles have steamed, remove the stems, and peel and discard the blackened skin. Place the roasted jalapeños in a food processor or blender. Add the tomatillos, avocado, cilantro, vinegar, and ¼ tsp salt. Purée until smooth, and adjust the salt to taste. Use immediately.

This is a "dry" salsa, a mix of seeds, nuts, and chiles, stirred with just enough oil to bring it together. It's inspired by a favorite *antojitos* (appetizers) spot that used to be in the Boyle Heights neighborhood of L.A. Antojitos Carmen was known for its Mexico City–style huaraches and a couple of hot, hot salsas. One was a habanero salsa and the other was owner Carmen Castellanos's dry salsa. Like Carmen's, our version at Bar Amá includes pumpkin seeds, sesame seeds, and tepin chiles, but we like to add pine nuts to the mix and nutritional yeast for its umami. Sprinkle it on steamed vegetables, roast fish, and tacos, and stir it into soups and salsas.

NOTE : You can substitute dried arbol or pequín chiles for dried tepin chiles.

MAKES ABOUT 1½ CUPS (170 G)

2 ½ tsp olive oil, plus more as needed

2 garlic cloves, finely chopped

2 or 3 dried tepin chiles

½ cup [60 g] pine nuts

½ cup [70 g] pumpkin seeds

¼ cup [35 g] toasted white sesame seeds

1 ½ Tbsp nutritional yeast

¾ tsp garlic powder

¾ tsp Amá spice mix (page 32) or chile powder

Fine sea salt

Heat 1 tsp of the olive oil in a medium skillet over medium-high heat and toast the garlic and chiles until just fragrant, about 30 seconds. Add the pine nuts and pumpkin seeds and toast, stirring frequently, until fragrant, about 2 minutes. Add the sesame seeds and toast until fragrant and golden brown, 1 to 2 minutes. Everything in the pan should be toasty and golden at this point. Be careful not to burn.

Remove from the heat and cool to room temperature. Add the nutritional yeast, garlic powder, and spice mix. Grind the mixture with a mortar and pestle or a food processor. It should be a coarse mixture. Transfer to a bowl or container and add just enough olive oil so that it comes together, about 1½ tsp. Add salt to taste. Use immediately or store in a covered container in a cool, dark place for up to 1 week.

We make this all-purpose smoky, earthy, savory chile paste for marinating chicken at Bar Amá and smear it all over the birds before roasting. It's inspired by a family recipe from my longtime friend and Bar Amá prep chef, Salvador Vasquez. Salvador calls it *cobjini*, a word from one of the many Zapotec languages. (It's also known as *chintextle*.) We use guajillo chiles, hoja santa, cumin, garlic, and onion. Sometimes we add tomatillo for its tartness. It's great for all poultry, and you can add it to sauces such as moles and to soups. You can even use it as a meat or seafood marinade.

MAKES ABOUT 1½ CUPS (360 ML)

7 guajillo chiles

3 Tbsp olive oil

¼ medium white onion

5 garlic cloves, thinly sliced

1 Tbsp ground cumin

2 tsp dried hoja santa leaves (see Note, page 21)

1 cup [240 ml] water

¾ tsp fine sea salt

Heat the oven to 350°F [180°C].

Put the chiles on a baking sheet and toast in the oven until fragrant and brittle, about 10 minutes. Remove from the oven and cool. Remove the stems and seeds and tear into large pieces with your hands (I recommend wearing gloves). Set aside.

Heat 1 Tbsp of the olive oil in a medium skillet over medium-high heat until hot and shimmering. Add the onion and cook until light golden brown, about 3 minutes. Add the garlic and cook until fragrant, less than 1 minute.

Add the chiles, cumin, hoja santa, and ½ cup [120 ml] of the water and cook for 1 minute more. Remove from the heat and cool slightly.

Put the onion and chile mixture in a blender along with the remaining ½ cup [120 ml] of water and blend to a smooth purée. Transfer to a medium bowl and stir in the remaining 2 Tbsp of olive oil and the salt. Store, covered, in the refrigerator for up to 4 days.

TOMATILLO COBJINI

Roast 3 husked and rinsed tomatillos in the oven along with the chiles until charred and softened, about 10 minutes; set aside. Proceed with the recipe, and add the tomatillos to the blender with the onion and chile mixture.

My mom made tomatillo salsa for enchiladas. Tangy, spicy, and versatile, it was one of the first sauces I learned to make. Use the salsa for chips, tacos, and eggs and tortillas, or warm it and serve it over albondigas (page 86).

MAKES ABOUT 1 CUP (240 ML)

14 oz [400 g] tomatillos, husked and rinsed

2 serrano chiles

1 large shallot

3 garlic cloves

Fine sea salt

½ bunch fresh cilantro, leaves and soft stems

Heat the broiler.

Put the tomatillos, chiles, shallot, and garlic on a foil-lined baking sheet and sprinkle with a pinch of salt. Broil until the vegetables are charred and softened, 3 to 5 minutes, flipping over with tongs halfway through cooking. Remove from the oven and cool slightly.

Put the roasted vegetables in a food processor or blender, add the cilantro and ½ tsp salt, and process to a coarse purée. Taste and add more salt, if desired. Transfer to a small bowl and serve immediately, or store, covered, in the refrigerator for up to 2 days.

Charred green onions were the stuff of every family barbecue, served with steaks or ribs or fajitas. And there would always be crema or sour cream. This recipe combines the two.

MAKES 1 CUP (240 ML)

4 green onions
1 cup [240 g] crème fraîche or crema Mexicana
Pinch of fine sea salt

Roast the green onions over the open flame of a gas burner or medium-hot grill, turning frequently, until charred, 3 to 4 minutes.

Finely chop the charred green onions (white and green parts), and transfer to a medium bowl. Add the crema and salt and stir until thoroughly combined. Store, covered, in the refrigerator for up to 2 days.

KEY LIME CREMA

Replace the roasted green onions with the zest of 3 key limes and the juice of ½ key lime.

I remember pimento spread as a kid. My grandpa would smear it on toast or stuff it into the valleys of celery sticks. Although my grandpa's spread came from a jar, I now take pimento cheese— "the pâté of the South"—more seriously. We make it at Bar Amá as a dip, and we stuff chiles and squash blossoms with it, too. It's also great on sandwiches or crackers, of course, and in quesadillas. Our recipe is cheesy and creamy thanks to the cream cheese and crème fraîche. And we add a lot of stuff—Tabasco and Worcestershire sauce and chile, onion, and garlic powders. Diced pickle (and sometimes a spoonful of pickle juice) add a pop.

MAKES 2½ CUPS (570 G)

1 cascabel chile

5 piquillo peppers, stemmed and finely chopped

6 oz [170 g] cream cheese

¼ cup [60 g] crème fraîche or crema Mexicana

1 Tbsp mayonnaise

1 dash of Tabasco

1 dash of Worcestershire sauce

1 tsp onion powder

1 tsp garlic powder

1 tsp Amá spice mix (page 32) or chile powder

3 Tbsp diced cheddar cheese

3 Tbsp diced Swiss cheese

1 small dill pickle, finely diced

2 Tbsp chopped fresh chives

Using tongs, toast the cascabel chile over the open flame of a gas burner until slightly softened and fragrant, 1 to 2 minutes. Grind to a powder with a spice grinder or mortar and pestle. Set aside.

Put the piquillo peppers in a food processor and pulse a few times to break them down a bit. Add the cream cheese, crème fraîche, mayonnaise, Tabasco, Worcestershire sauce, ground cascabel chile, onion powder, garlic powder, and spice mix, and pulse to incorporate. Add the cheddar cheese and pulse again a few times. Add the Swiss cheese and pulse just until combined. The mixture shouldn't be too smooth or too chunky.

Transfer the pimento cheese mixture to a medium bowl and fold in the diced pickle and chives. Refrigerate for about 1 hour before using. Store in a covered container in the refrigerator for up to 2 days.

MEX

BREAKFAST

Migas literally means "crumbs," which are traditionally crushed tortilla chips served with scrambled eggs (and not to be confused with chilaquiles). I learned how to prepare migas by watching my mom, who made it on Saturday or Sunday mornings. She would cut up tortilla strips and fry them until supercrispy; that was key. The eggs are cooked just enough to suspend the chips, so they stay crisp. It happens fast, in a minute or less.

SERVES 4

5 eggs

1 Tbsp milk

¼ tsp fine sea salt

¼ cup [60 ml] olive or avocado oil

Three 6 in [15 cm] corn tortillas, cut into 1 ½ in [4 cm] squares

1 medium russet or large red potato, cut into ⅛ in [4 mm] slices (optional)

¼ cup plus 1 Tbsp [40 g] finely chopped onion

2 garlic cloves, grated with a rasp-style grater

1 serrano chile, stemmed, seeded, and chopped

¼ cup [25 g] finely grated cheddar cheese

1 Tbsp chopped fresh cilantro leaves

4 tsp sour cream

1 Tbsp soldadera's hot sauce (page 34) or your favorite hot sauce

In a medium bowl, whisk together the eggs, milk, and salt and set aside.

Heat the oil in a large skillet over high heat until shimmering and hot. It should sizzle when you drop in the tortillas. Add the tortillas and potatoes, if using, and cook, stirring briskly, until the tortillas are toasted, 3 to 4 minutes. Add ¼ cup [30 g] of the onion and the garlic and sauté until the onions are caramelized slightly, 2 to 3 minutes. Add the serrano, and remove from the heat. Drain and discard the excess oil.

Return the pan to high heat (it should be very hot so that the eggs cook quickly and the tortillas stay crispy). Add the whisked egg mixture and cook, stirring constantly with a heat-proof rubber spatula, just until the eggs are cooked through, 45 seconds to 1 minute.

Divide the egg mixture among four plates and top each one with some of the cheese, remaining 1 Tbsp onion, cilantro, sour cream, and hot sauce. Serve immediately.

I can still see Grandma Alice sitting in a corner booth at the Pig Stand on Broadway—a small San Antonio diner in the shadow of the I-35 overpass. She's with a few friends, gambling old ladies who sometimes show up for a morning round of Bunco. My brother, Aramis, and I are sitting at the bar eating huevos rancheros with bacon. But mostly we're there for the free-flowing quarters from Grandma Alice so we can play the one arcade game in the place—*Kung-Fu Master*.

SERVES 4

1½ cups [510 g] crushed San Marzano tomatoes,
or 3 ripe Roma tomatoes, coarsely chopped

¼ medium white onion

1 serrano chile

½ tsp dried Mexican oregano, preferably Oregano Indio (see Note, page 17)

½ tsp chile powder

2 to 3 Tbsp water, as needed

½ cup plus 1 Tbsp [135 ml] olive or avocado oil

1 garlic clove, finely chopped

Fine sea salt

Four 6 in [15 cm] corn tortillas

4 eggs

Refried borracho beans (page 147), reheated if necessary

1 lime, quartered

Fresh cilantro leaves for garnish

Sliced green onions (green part only) for garnish

Put the tomatoes, onion, serrano chile, oregano, and chile powder in a blender and blend into a smooth purée, adding the water if needed.

Heat 1 Tbsp of the oil in a saucepan over medium heat and sweat the garlic until fragrant (it shouldn't color), 10 to 20 seconds.

Carefully pour the contents of the blender into the saucepan. Bring to a simmer and continue simmering until the salsa is deep red in color and has thickened slightly, about 10 minutes. Season with 1 tsp salt and keep warm while you fry the tortillas.

Pour the remaining ½ cup [120 ml] of oil into a medium skillet. The oil should come up the sides of the pan about ¼ in [6 mm]. Heat the oil over medium-high heat. Fry the tortillas, one at a time, for about 10 seconds on each side. Don't allow the tortillas to harden; you want them chewy-crispy. Transfer to a paper towel–lined platter and set aside.

Use the remaining oil to cook the eggs, sunny-side up: Heat the oil over medium heat. When it's hot, add 2 of the eggs to the oil. Cook until the whites are just cooked through and the yolks are still runny. Transfer to a plate and cover with aluminum foil. Fry the remaining 2 eggs.

Place a tortilla on each of four plates. Smear each one with a heaping spoonful of borracho beans. Gently place an egg on top of the beans. Spoon some of the warm salsa over each egg. Squeeze with a lime quarter and garnish with cilantro and green onions. Serve immediately.

Kielbasa (a popular sausage in central Texas) is one of my favorite breakfast taco fillings. It's also great in a hash or scramble. Here the sliced sausage is added to eggs, onions, and potatoes and served on a fresh tortilla with some salsa.

SERVES 6

1 pasilla de Oaxaca or dried New Mexico chile

1 ½ lb [680 g] fingerling potatoes, cut in half crosswise or, if long, cut into quarters

1 Tbsp distilled white vinegar

Fine sea salt

5 Tbsp [60 ml] olive or avocado or olive oil, plus more as needed

4 oz [115 g] kielbasa, sliced

Fresh black pepper

¼ yellow onion, diced

2 garlic cloves, minced

1 cipollini onion, finely chopped, green part reserved for garnish

1 serrano chile, stemmed, seeded, and chopped

3 eggs, lightly beaten with a fork

¼ cup [7 g] chopped fresh cilantro leaves

½ small avocado, diced

½ cup [120 ml] Mexican salmorejo (page 28), tomatillo salsa (page 43), or your favorite hot sauce (optional)

6 flour or corn tortillas (any size), warmed in a skillet over medium heat

Using tongs, toast the dried chile over the open flame of a gas burner until slightly softened and fragrant, 1 to 2 minutes. Cool slightly, then remove the stem and seeds, tear the chile into small pieces, and set aside.

Put the potatoes in a medium pot and cover with water. Add the vinegar and 2 Tbsp salt, and bring to a boil over high heat. Lower the heat and simmer until barely tender, about 5 minutes. Drain the potatoes in a colander for at least 2 minutes, and set aside.

Heat 1 Tbsp of the oil in a skillet over medium-high heat. Add the sausage and cook, stirring, until crisp on both sides and the fat has rendered out, about 8 minutes. Remove with a slotted spoon to a large bowl and set aside.

Discard the fat from the skillet. When the potatoes are drained and dry, add 3 Tbsp oil to the pan and heat over medium-high heat. Add the potatoes and cook, stirring and tossing occasionally, until crisp on all sides, 10 to 15 minutes.

Add the toasted chile and cook, stirring, until fragrant, about 30 seconds. Season with salt and pepper. Transfer the potatoes to the bowl with the sausage and set aside.

CONT'D

Add the remaining 1 Tbsp oil to the skillet and heat over high heat until hot and shimmering. Add the onion, garlic, chopped white part of the cippolini, and the serrano chile and cook, stirring occasionally, until browned, about 2 minutes. Season with salt and pepper.

Return the potato and sausage mixture to the skillet, and lower the heat to medium-high. Add the beaten eggs to the pan and cook, stirring, until the eggs are set, 2 to 3 minutes. Remove from the heat, and garnish with the sliced cipollini greens, chopped cilantro, and avocado. Serve immediately with salsa, if using, and tortillas.

Texas is known for its red grapefruits from the Rio Grande Valley, like Ruby Red and Ruby Rio. My tía (aunt) Joann especially liked them. She would split them, cut around the segments, brush them with a little butter, and sprinkle them with sugar before putting them under the broiler. They're sweet, tart, warm, and juicy.

NOTE : Piloncillo, available at Latino markets, is raw cane sugar, which is sold in solid cones. Because the sugar hasn't been processed, it has a golden brown color and rich molasses flavor. To use piloncillo, grate the cone on the largest holes of a box grater, or use a sharp serrated knife to scrape the sugar off the edges of the cone and finely chop. (If the piloncillo is very hard, you can soften it in the microwave for 10 to 20 seconds first.)

SERVES 4

2 *Ruby Red or other red grapefruit*

3 *Tbsp grated piloncillo or brown sugar*

¼ *tsp ground cinnamon*

1 *Tbsp melted unsalted butter*

Position a rack about 6 in [15 cm] from the broiler, and heat the broiler. Line a baking sheet with aluminum foil.

Cut the grapefruits in half across the equator. Trim a thin slice off the bottom of each half so the halves sit flat. Remove any seeds and, using a paring knife, cut around each segment so it's loosened from the pith and peel. Put the grapefruit halves on the prepared baking sheet.

Stir together the piloncillo sugar and cinnamon in a small bowl. Brush some of the melted butter over the top of each grapefruit half, and sprinkle with 1½ tsp of the piloncillo mixture in an even layer.

Broil the grapefruit until the tops are bubbling and golden brown, 8 to 10 minutes, being careful not to burn the sugar and rotating the baking sheet halfway through cooking. Remove from the oven and serve immediately.

Fresh flour tortillas were always a must-have in my family. Every Sunday we would pick up a batch from Taxco Tamale and Tortilla Factory. There were often lines for Mr. and Mrs. Copado's soft, fluffy, chewy tortillas, and my brother and I would eat them out of the bag in the car on the way home. Now I make them myself, using the recipe of my tía Carmen, who taught generations of the Centeno family how to make tortillas. The milk makes the dough easy to work with. And rolling them out is a cinch. Warm tortillas straight from the pan or griddle are the best.

MAKES SIX 8 IN (20 CM) TORTILLAS

1 cup [135 g] all-purpose flour, plus more for dusting

1 Tbsp lard, shortening, or rendered bacon fat

½ tsp baking powder

½ tsp fine sea salt

½ cup [120 ml] whole milk

Put the flour, lard, baking powder, and salt in the bowl of a stand mixer fitted with the dough hook. Mix at low speed just until incorporated.

Warm the milk in a small saucepan over medium heat until it begins to steam (make sure it doesn't boil). With the mixer on medium-low speed, pour the warm milk into the flour mixture, and mix until the milk is completely absorbed by the dry ingredients and the dough forms a rough ball and separates from the bowl. It will happen fast, in about 20 seconds. Shape the dough into a smoother ball (it will be soft and slightly lumpy on the surface).

Transfer the dough to a lightly oiled medium bowl, cover, and let rest in a warm place for 30 minutes and up to 1 hour.

Heat a skillet or griddle on medium-low heat. Uncover the dough and divide into six 1½ oz [40 g] balls. Generously flour a smooth work surface and roll out each ball into an 8 in [20 cm] circle.

Use a paper towel to lightly oil the hot pan, and gently place a tortilla on it. Cook until bubbles form on the entire surface of the tortilla, about 1 minute, and flip.

The tortilla will start to leaven once flipped. When the leavening stops and the tortilla is golden brown on the bottom, about 1 minute, remove from the heat and transfer to a plate. Repeat with the remaining dough. Serve immediately.

THE FIRST TACO OF THE DAY

I grew up on breakfast tacos. Texas breakfast tacos. More specifically, tortillas (usually flour) filled with either American diner ingredients like scrambled eggs and sausage or Mexican deliciousness like barbacoa. I thought of them as an easy way to eat breakfast without a plate. You can't really eat bacon and eggs in a car on your way to school—but you can if they're in a taco.

The debate over where the Tex-Mex breakfast taco originated or which city popularized it— San Antonio or Austin—I didn't know this existed until fairly recently. If you grow up in S.A., why would you think to question things like where the Alamo is or where breakfast tacos come from? Regarding the latter, if not San Antonio, then Corpus Christi? Again, as a kid, I didn't think about this. Most adults, especially non-Texans, probably don't either. And other than having been born and raised in Texas, I'm no expert. But Gustavo Arellano, award-winning columnist and author of the book *Ask a Mexican* (2008), made it pretty clear in an article on the subject, "Who Invented Breakfast Tacos? Not Austin—And People Should STFU About It."

Breakfast tacos became part of my morning routine when I was in elementary school. My dad drove my younger brother, Aramis, and me to San Antonio Academy every day. If we didn't meet Grandma Alice at Charles Pharmacy for breakfast, then we often stopped at the Original Donut Shop not far from school. It didn't matter if we were already running late (which we usually were). We made the stop anyway because my dad and Aramis were big on breakfast.

I wasn't a morning person, so I was barely awake when Dad's white Dodge pickup would roll into the parking lot. Around since the 1950s, the restaurant still regularly makes it onto "best breakfast tacos in San Antonio" lists. Dad would give us money, and Aramis and I would go in and order for the three of us.

This is how it worked, and still does, at the Original Donut Shop: There were two separate lines, one for the donuts and one for the tacos (the drive-through windows, which came later, work the same way). They don't sell tacos to you if you're in the donut line, and they don't sell donuts to you if you're in the taco line.

I'm pretty sure many of the same women from back then are working behind the counter today (forever sixty-five years old), some of them friends of Grandma Alice. The flour tortillas were—and are—made by hand, really thin but strong enough so they wouldn't tear (which is key when eating them in a car). One would roll the tortillas, another would throw them on the comal, and a third would fill them. They always knew our order: whatever donut was hot out of the fryer for my dad and Aramis, and a carne guisada breakfast taco for me.

Everybody I know has a different favorite breakfast taco: breakfast sausage and egg; barbacoa with avocado and salt; bean and cheese with bacon, chilaquiles, and *machacado* (shredded beef); or carne guisada, which is still my favorite. It is a no-frills breakfast taco— a flour tortilla and a couple of spoonfuls of carne guisada, a simple Tejano stew of beef with onion, tomatoes, and chiles. This breakfast taco filling is perfect on its own. No eggs, salsa, or cheese necessary.

Carne guisada is my "bowl of red," except I never eat it in a bowl—always in a flour tortilla. Like chili con carne, this stewed beef is made with chunks of beef and dried chiles and spices, and it also contains tomatoes. But unlike chili con carne, it isn't served with a bunch of other ingredients and garnishes. Tucked into a flour tortilla, it needs nothing else—just straight up carne guisada.

SERVES 6 TO 8

2 ancho chiles

4 Tbsp [60 ml] olive or avocado oil

2 ½ to 3 lb [1.2 to 1.4 kg] boneless short rib, trimmed and cut into 1 ½ in [4 cm] cubes

1 large onion, finely diced

½ tsp fine sea salt

5 garlic cloves, chopped

1 serrano chile, stemmed, seeded, and finely chopped

1 Tbsp dried Mexican oregano, preferably Oregano Indio (see Note, page 17)

1 ½ tsp cumin seeds

1 tsp chile powder

1 fresh bay leaf, or 2 dried

Fresh black pepper

2 Tbsp all-purpose flour

3 cups [720 ml] beef broth

1 cup [340 g] crushed San Marzano tomatoes

Using tongs, toast the ancho chiles over the open flame of a gas burner until slightly softened and fragrant, 1 to 2 minutes. Stem and seed the chiles and tear them into pieces. Set aside.

Heat 2 Tbsp of the oil in a Dutch oven or another large heavy-bottom pot over medium-high heat. When the oil shimmers, add the beef and brown it on all sides, 10 to 12 minutes.

Add the remaining 2 Tbsp of oil to the pot. When the oil is hot, add the onion and salt and cook over medium heat, scraping up the browned bits of meat at the bottom of the pot, until the onions are soft, about 5 minutes. Add the garlic, serrano, oregano, cumin seeds, chile powder, bay leaf, and several grinds of black pepper and cook until fragrant, 30 seconds.

Add the toasted chiles to the pot along with the flour and stir until incorporated. Add the beef broth and tomatoes and bring the mixture to a boil.

Reduce the heat to low and simmer, partly covered, stirring occasionally, until the meat is tender and the sauce is thickened, 2 ½ to 3 hours. Taste and adjust the salt. Store, covered, in the refrigerator for up to 3 days.

Grandma Alice always had chorizo around. It was breakfast food for her (and for us when we visited)—along with melty cheese and fresh flour tortillas. Like all the Mexican chorizo I grew up with, Grandma Alice's was spiced fresh-ground pork with no casing. She cooked it and then added it to scrambled eggs, tacos, or queso. Her spice mix included the usual cumin, coriander, cloves, bay leaves, cinnamon, oregano, thyme, and paprika, along with a chile blend. Here, I use ground pork belly, and chipotle powder and Amá spice mix for the chile blend.

MAKES ABOUT 2 CUPS (340 G)

1 Tbsp cumin seed

1 tsp coriander seed

3 whole cloves

2 dried bay leaves

1 Tbsp chipotle chile powder

2 Tbsp Amá spice mix (page 32) or chile powder

2 Tbsp sweet paprika

1 tsp fine sea salt

1 tsp fresh black pepper

½ tsp dried Mexican oregano, preferably Oregano Indio (see Note, page 17)

½ tsp dried thyme

¼ tsp ground cinnamon

1½ lb [680 g] ground pork belly or ground pork shoulder

1 large garlic clove, grated with a rasp-style grater

3 Tbsp apple cider vinegar

Toast the cumin, coriander, and cloves in a small, dry skillet over medium heat, stirring frequently, until fragrant, 1 to 1½ minutes. Grind with a mortar and pestle or spice grinder to a fine powder.

With your fingers, break up the bay leaves into small pieces, add them to the spices, and grind to a fine powder. Add the chile powder, spice mix, paprika, salt, pepper, oregano, thyme, and cinnamon, and grind or stir until everything is well combined. Set aside.

Put the ground pork in a large bowl. Add the garlic, vinegar, and half of the spice mixture and, using your hands (I recommend wearing gloves), work it into the pork. Add the rest of the spice mixture and work it into the pork until fully incorporated and the meat is red from the spices.

If you have the time, let the chorizo sit, covered, in the refrigerator overnight, so the flavors come together.

Heat a large skillet over medium-high heat. Add the chorizo, breaking it up with a wooden spoon, and cook, stirring occasionally, until the meat is cooked through and crisped and the fat is rendered, 6 to 8 minutes. Use immediately or store in a covered container in the refrigerator for up to 3 days, or in the freezer for up to 1 month. (Thaw and reheat in a skillet over medium heat before serving).

A Tex-Mex standby, picadillo is made with ground beef, potatoes, onion, tomatoes, and spices. My tía Mona cooked this all the time and liked to serve it in tacos with chopped tomatoes, or on top of enchiladas. You can also serve it simply with rice or use it in taquitos, chalupas, or queso. When served along with eggs in a flour tortilla, it makes a great breakfast taco.

MAKES ABOUT 3 CUPS (750 G)

1 tsp olive oil

½ tsp cumin seeds

¼ medium yellow onion, finely diced

1 garlic clove, grated with a rasp-style grater or thinly sliced

¼ jalapeño, seeded and finely chopped

½ russet potato, peeled and cut into a ¼ in [6 mm] dice

1 lb [455 g] ground beef

1 ripe tomato, grated on the largest holes of a box grater, or 2 tsp tomato paste

¾ tsp fine sea salt

1 tsp smoked paprika

1 tsp Amá spice mix (page 32) or chile powder

¼ cup [20 g] chopped green onions (white and green parts)

¼ cup [7 g] chopped fresh cilantro leaves

Heat the olive oil in a large skillet over medium-high heat. Add the cumin seeds and let them sizzle for a few seconds. Add the onion and garlic and cook until fragrant, 1 minute. Add the jalapeño and cook, stirring occasionally, until the onion begins to brown, 2 to 3 minutes.

Add the diced potatoes and stir to combine. Add the ground beef, breaking it up with a wooden spoon. Lower the heat to medium, add the tomato and salt, and cook, stirring and breaking up the beef, until the beef is browned and the potatoes are cooked through, about 10 minutes.

Stir in the smoked paprika and spice mix until fully incorporated. Add the green onions and cilantro and remove from the heat. Use immediately or store in a covered container in the refrigerator for up to 2 days, or in the freezer for up to 1 month. (Thaw and reheat in a skillet over medium heat before serving.)

POTATO AND EGG BREAKFAST TACOS

6 oz [170 g] new potatoes (about 4)

2 Tbsp avocado oil

Fine sea salt

2 slices bacon, cut into ¼ in [6 mm] pieces (optional)

1 shallot, thinly sliced

1 serrano or fresh pequín chile, stemmed, seeded, and thinly sliced

3 eggs

1 Tbsp milk

Fresh black pepper

6 flour tortillas, homemade (page 59) or store-bought,
warmed in a skillet over medium heat

½ to 1 cup [50 to 100 g] finely grated cheddar cheese

Your favorite hot sauce for serving (optional)

Cut the potatoes in half lengthwise, and cut each half into ¼ in [6 mm] slices.

Heat the oil in a medium skillet over medium-high heat until hot and shimmering. Add the sliced potatoes and a pinch of salt and sauté until cooked through, about 5 minutes. Add the bacon, if using, and cook until the bacon is crisp, another 4 minutes.

Add the sliced shallot and chile and cook, stirring occasionally, for 1 to 2 minutes.

In a small bowl, beat the eggs lightly with a fork, add the milk and a pinch of salt, and beat again. Add the eggs to the pan and cook, stirring with a wooden spoon or heat-proof spatula, until set, 1 to 2 minutes. Remove from the heat, and season with a few grinds of black pepper.

Put a heaping spoonful of potato and egg mixture in the center of each tortilla. Sprinkle liberally with cheese. Serve immediately, with hot sauce on the side, if desired.

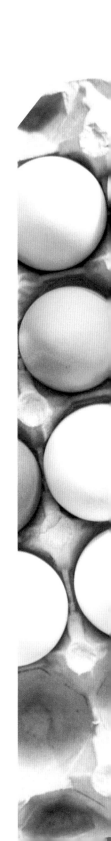

6 eggs

⅓ cup [25 g] chopped green onions (white and green parts)

¾ tsp fine sea salt

1 tsp olive oil

1 ½ cups [375 g] Tía Mona's picadillo (page 66) or Grandma Alice's chipotle chorizo (page 65)

6 flour tortillas, homemade (page 59) or store-bought, warmed in a skillet over medium heat

½ cup [50 g] grated cheddar cheese

¼ head iceberg lettuce, cut into shreds

½ cup [120 g] crema Mexicana or sour cream (optional)

Your favorite hot sauce for serving

In a medium bowl, whisk together the eggs, green onions, and salt.

Heat the oil in a skillet over medium heat until hot and shimmering. Add the picadillo and eggs and cook, stirring constantly, until the eggs are set, about 2 minutes. Remove from the heat.

Divide the egg mixture among the flour tortillas. Top with cheddar cheese, lettuce, and crema, if using, and fold. Serve immediately with hot sauce.

BEAN, CHEESE, AND BACON BREAKFAST TACOS

6 slices bacon

2 cups borracho beans (page 145) or refried borracho beans (page 147)

⅛ tsp Amá spice mix (page 32) or chile powder

Fine sea salt

Fresh black pepper

1 serrano chile or fresh pequín, stemmed, seeded, and finely chopped (optional)

6 flour tortillas, homemade (page 59) or store-bought, warmed in a skillet over medium heat

1 cup [100 g] finely grated cheddar cheese

Fresh cilantro leaves for garnish

Your favorite hot sauce for serving

Cook the bacon in a medium skillet over medium heat until the fat renders out and the bacon is crispy on the edges. Transfer to a plate lined with paper towels to drain.

Put the beans in a medium saucepan over medium heat, add the spice mix, salt, pepper, and the serrano, if using, and warm the beans, stirring occasionally, until they're hot and bubbly. Keep warm.

Place a heaping spoon of beans in the center of each tortilla. Add a slice of bacon, sprinkle liberally with cheese, and fold. Serve immediately with cilantro leaves and hot sauce.

The first biscuits and gravy I ever had was probably at a Luby's Cafeteria, a chain that started in San Antonio. All of my grandparents were probably regulars. It would have been a soft, fluffy biscuit split in half and covered with a smooth blanket of white gravy. Where warm biscuit met warm gravy, there would be an indistinguishable layer that was neither distinctly biscuit nor distinctly gravy. The gravy was kind of flavorless but comforting. I don't make that. I add bacon, onion, garlic, and chile, which give the gravy a lot of flavor. To get moist, layered biscuits, I make the dough with cream and buttermilk , and work plenty of cold butter into the flour.

SERVES 6

Biscuits

3 ⅓ cups [450 g] all-purpose flour

2 Tbsp sugar

2 Tbsp baking powder

1 tsp fine sea salt

1 cup [220 g] cold unsalted butter, cut into ¼ in [6 mm] slices

¾ cup [180 ml] cold heavy cream, plus more for brushing

½ cup [120 ml] buttermilk

1 egg, lightly beaten

Bacon gravy

1 Tbsp unsalted butter

1 Tbsp all-purpose flour

3 slices bacon, cut into ½ in [12 mm] pieces

¼ cup [30 g] finely chopped yellow onion

3 garlic cloves, minced

2 cups [480 ml] milk

1 tsp fine sea salt

Fresh black pepper

1 tsp Amá spice mix (page 32) or chile powder

MAKE THE BISCUITS: Heat the oven to 400°F [200°C].

Combine the flour, sugar, baking powder, and salt in a large bowl and whisk together. Add the cold butter. Using your fingers, pinch the pieces of butter and flour together so that you get uneven shards and beads of butter (don't work the butter for long).

Make a well in the middle, pour in the cream and buttermilk, and stir to combine. With your fingers, fold the dry ingredients into the wet ones just until combined. The dough will be moist and pretty crumbly; press it into a small rectangle and cover with plastic wrap. Refrigerate for 1 hour.

CONT'D

Remove the dough from the refrigerator and transfer to a work surface. With a rolling pin, gently roll out the dough into a 7 by 10 in [17 by 25 cm] rectangle, ¾ to 1 in [2 to 2.5 cm] thick. With a biscuit cutter, cut out six 3 in [7.5 cm] round biscuits, and place on a baking sheet.

Brush the biscuits with the beaten egg. Bake for 10 minutes. Lower the heat to 350°F [180°C] and continue baking until the biscuits are golden brown, have risen slightly, and have visible layers, about 20 minutes longer. Cool the biscuits slightly, and cut them in half horizontally.

WHILE THE BISCUITS ARE BAKING, MAKE THE BACON GRAVY: In a small bowl, knead the butter and flour together.

Cook the bacon in a heavy-bottom skillet over medium-high heat until the fat renders and the edges are just browned (the bacon will still be soft), 3 to 5 minutes. Add the onion and garlic and sauté until the onion is translucent, 2 to 3 minutes. Whisk in the milk, salt, a few grinds of black pepper, and the spice mix.

Whisk in the butter-flour mixture all at once and cook, stirring frequently, until the gravy is nappe (coats the back of a spoon) and there is no raw-flour taste, about 5 minutes. Keep warm.

Place the bottom half of each biscuit on a plate. Spoon over the bacon gravy and cover with the top half of the biscuit. Serve immediately.

Apá, my great-grandfather on my mom's side, loved cornbread—it was one of the few things he cooked. My mom adapted his recipe to make cornmeal pancakes, which she served with lots of butter and syrup that was part molasses and part maple. Bar Amá serves a version of it with pecans or sometimes berries when they're in season, along with whipped butter.

SERVES 4

1½ cups [360 ml] maple syrup

½ cup [160 g] molasses

½ cup [110 g] unsalted butter, plus 4 to 5 Tbsp [55 to 70 g] more for cooking and serving

1 cup [160 g] fine polenta, preferably Anson Mills

½ cup [70 g] all-purpose flour

½ cup [65 g] pastry flour

1 tsp fine sea salt

½ tsp baking soda

¼ tsp baking powder

1⅓ cups [320 ml] buttermilk

¼ cup [50 g] sugar

2 Tbsp honey

2 eggs

Toasted pecans or fresh berries for garnish

Put the maple syrup and molasses in a small saucepan and heat over medium heat, stirring, for 2 to 3 minutes. Set aside. In another small saucepan or microwave-safe bowl, melt ½ cup [110 g] of the butter.

In a large bowl, whisk together the polenta, flours, salt, baking soda, and baking powder. Add the buttermilk, melted butter, sugar, honey, and eggs and stir until smooth. Chill the batter in the refrigerator for 20 minutes.

Heat 1 Tbsp butter in a large nonstick skillet over medium-high heat. When the butter is melted and foaming, ladle the pancake batter into the pan, about ½ cup [120 ml] for each pancake. Cook until air bubbles form on top and the bottom is toasted brown, 2 to 3 minutes. Flip the pancakes over and cook 2 to 3 minutes, until the pancakes are cooked through and the bottom is browned. Repeat with the remaining batter.

Garnish the pancakes with toasted pecans. Serve immediately with the maple-molasses syrup and butter.

My mom made French toast from a big bag of Texas toast—those extra-thick slices often used for garlic bread. It was usually ButterKrust, made right in San Antonio. I remember its '40s-era Art Deco headquarters with its big billboard, featuring rotating slices of bread. It was the kind of bread everybody grew up on—fluffy, soft, and white. Now I make French toast with brioche or pain de mie—but I still cut the slices thick, Texas-toast size.

SERVES 4

6 eggs

¾ cup [180 ml] half-and-half or whole milk

2 Tbsp grated piloncillo (see Note, page 58)
or dark brown sugar

1 tsp ground cinnamon

Seeds of 1 vanilla pod

Eight 1 in [2.5 cm] thick slices of soft-crusted bread,
such as a brioche loaf, preferably day old

¼ cup [55 g] unsalted butter, plus more, at room temperature, for serving

Warm maple syrup or pure honey for serving

Toasted pecans for garnish (optional)

Beat the eggs, half-and-half, piloncillo, cinnamon, and vanilla seeds in a large, shallow dish, such as a 9 by 13 in [23 by 33 cm] baking dish. Add the bread and turn to coat so that it absorbs the egg mixture.

Melt the butter in large, heavy skillet over medium heat. Add the bread and cook until golden brown and cooked through, about 3 minutes per side. (If you have to do this in batches, add more butter to the pan.) Transfer to plates. Serve immediately with maple syrup, butter, and pecans, if using.

AMÁ

S
TABLE

This is loosely based on a family chicken soup recipe. Mama Grande, my great-grandmother on my dad's side, would kill and butcher a chicken at the ranch and put on a pot of chicken soup and rice with lots of cilantro. It probably resembles everybody's grandma's soup—simple and comforting, not too spicy, and good for a hot lunch or when you feel like you're coming down with a cold. We'll make it for staff meal at Amá and call the whole pot of it the *abuelita*, or "granny." As in, "Just throw that in the *abuelita*."

SERVES 6

2 Tbsp olive oil

1 large onion, coarsely chopped

1 head garlic, peeled and coarsely chopped

3 large celery stalks, cut into ¼ in [6 mm] slices,
plus the leaves of 1 bunch celery, chopped

1 cup [200 g] long-grain brown rice

One 3½ to 4 lb [1.6 to 1.8 kg] chicken,
cut into 8 pieces (legs, thighs, breasts, and wings)

1 cup [15 g] fresh cilantro leaves, chopped, plus extra for garnish

8 cups [2 L] water

Fresh black pepper

Fine sea salt

3 Tbsp sliced green onions (green part only) for garnish

1 Tbsp toasted white sesame seeds for garnish

2 limes, cut into wedges for garnish

Heat the oil in a large pot or Dutch oven over medium-high heat until hot and shimmering. Add the onion, garlic, and celery stalks and cook, stirring, for 2 minutes. Add the rice and give it a stir.

Add the chicken pieces, celery leaves, and cilantro. Add the water and bring to a boil. Reduce the heat to medium-low, cover, and simmer, skimming off the fat as needed, for 1 hour.

Add several grinds of pepper, taste, and add salt, if necessary.

If you want to remove the bones from the chicken, transfer the chicken pieces to a colander. When cool enough to handle, remove the skin and separate the meat from the bones. Discard the skin and bones, and return the chicken to the soup.

Serve in bowls, garnished with the green onions, sesame seeds, and lime wedges.

Grandma Alice made menudo for holidays; other days, she cooked this chicken tortilla soup. She made the same base for both, thick with tomatoes, tomatillos, onions, and chiles—roasted fresh poblanos and dried anchos. In her tortilla soup, she included plenty of chicken but no softened tortillas—just crispy-fried strips piled on each serving as a garnish.

SERVES 8

2 poblano chiles

3 ancho chiles

¼ cup plus 2 Tbsp [90 ml] avocado oil

Four 6 in [15 cm] corn tortillas,
halved and cut crosswise into ¼ in [6 mm] strips

Leaves of 1 large bunch fresh cilantro

1 onion, finely chopped

4 garlic cloves, peeled and smashed

1 serrano chile, stemmed, seeded, and sliced

1 Tbsp chile powder

2 tsp cumin seeds

1 tsp coriander seeds

8 cups chicken broth

6 tomatillos, husked, rinsed, and chopped (about 1 ½ cups [250 g])

1 ½ cups [510 g] crushed San Marzano tomatoes

1 fresh bay leaf, or 2 dried

2 ½ tsp fine sea salt

1 ¾ lb [800 g] boneless, skinless chicken thighs,
cut into ¾ in [2 cm] pieces

1 avocado, cut into ½ in [12 mm] dice

4 oz [115 g] cheddar cheese, grated

½ cup [120 g] crema Mexicana or sour cream

3 radishes, sliced into thin planks

Lime wedges (optional)

Roast each poblano chile by placing it directly over the open flame of a gas burner, turning it with tongs until the skin is charred all over, 1 to 2 minutes per side. Transfer to a large bowl and cover with plastic wrap; set aside to steam for 10 minutes. (Don't let them steam for too long, or they'll start to turn brown.) Rub off the charred skins with your fingers, and remove the stems, seeds, and veins (wear gloves, if you like). Chop into 1 in [2.5 cm] pieces and set aside.

Toast the ancho chiles over a burner the same way until slightly softened and fragrant, about 1 minute. Remove the stems and seeds. Tear them into small pieces and set aside.

CONT'D

In a large, heavy-bottom pot, heat the oil over medium-high heat. Fry half the tortilla strips in the hot oil, stirring, until golden and crispy, 1 to 2 minutes. Remove with a slotted spoon and drain on paper towels. Repeat with the other half of the tortilla strips. Set aside. Coarsely chop the cilantro leaves and set aside 3 Tbsp for garnish.

Lower the heat to medium-low. Add the onion, garlic, serrano chile, chile powder, cumin seeds, and coriander seeds. Cook, stirring, for 5 minutes. Add the broth, tomatillos, tomatoes, poblano and ancho chiles, cilantro, bay leaf, and salt. Bring to a simmer. Cook, uncovered, for 30 minutes; remove the bay leaf.

Add the chicken, return the soup to a simmer, and continue simmering until the chicken is just cooked through, about 2 minutes.

Serve the soup in bowls, and pass the avocado, cheddar, crema, radishes, the reserved 3 Tbsp chopped cilantro, the tortilla strips, and lime wedges, if using.

Grandma Alice liked to make chorizo with queso asadero—her version of queso fundido ("molten cheese")—for a snack or for breakfast, because everybody loved it so much. Who doesn't like a panful of melted cheese with crisped chorizo? She would fry up some chorizo in a small skillet, sprinkle over the cheese, and put it in the oven until the cheese was melted and bubbling. We'd eat it with tortilla chips or in a tortilla. At breakfast, she served it with café con leche.

NOTE : Queso asadero (also called queso quesadilla) is available at Latino markets; you can substitute quesillo (also called queso Oaxaca), Monterey Jack, or Fontina.

SERVES 4

½ cup [80 g] Grandma Alice's chipotle chorizo (page 65)

4 oz [115 g] queso asadero, grated

¼ cup [30 g] finely chopped red onion

¼ cup (7 g) finely chopped fresh cilantro leaves

½ lime

6 flour or corn tortillas, warmed in a skillet over medium heat

Heat a medium skillet over medium-high heat. Add the chorizo and heat until sizzling, about 2 minutes. Sprinkle the grated queso asadero over the chorizo, stir until the cheese starts to melt, and remove from the heat. Transfer to a serving dish.

Scatter the onion and cilantro on top and squeeze the lime over all. Serve immediately with the tortillas.

These tender beef and pork meatballs are flavored with oregano, garlic, chipotle, and caraway seeds, which Amá liked. Hers were bound with leftover rice, but I use panko. The quesillo makes these extra cheesy, and the grated cotija cheese adds texture, too. The meatballs should be moist (easily cut into with a spoon), but firm enough so that they don't fall apart. Serve them with warmed tomatillo salsa.

SERVES 4 TO 6

1 tsp caraway seeds, or 1 generous tsp ground caraway

⅓ cup [80 ml] milk

2 eggs

2 Tbsp chopped chipotle in adobo

½ cup [50 g] finely grated cotija cheese

4 oz [115 g] quesillo (also called queso Oaxaca) or Monterey Jack, cut into a small dice

2 tsp dried Mexican oregano, preferably Oregano Indio (see Note, page 17)

3 garlic cloves, minced

1 tsp fine sea salt

⅓ cup [20 g] panko

1 lb [455 g] ground beef

1 lb [455 g] ground pork

⅓ to ½ cup [80 to 120 ml] water

Tomatillo salsa (page 43), warmed, for serving

Heat the oven to 400°F [200°C].

Toast the caraway seeds in a small, dry skillet, stirring frequently, until fragrant, 1 to 2 minutes. Grind to a fine powder with a mortar and pestle or spice grinder. Set aside.

Whisk together the milk, eggs, and chipotle in a medium bowl. Add the cheeses, oregano, garlic, and salt, and mix thoroughly. Stir in the panko.

Put the beef and pork in a large bowl, add the egg mixture, and combine gently, using one hand and a rubber spatula (the other hand stays clean in case you need to reach for something). Be careful not to overwork the mixture. Add the water as needed to lighten the meatball mixture, but not too much or you won't be able to form the meatballs.

Form the meatballs with a 2½ oz (70 g) ice cream scoop (you could also weigh them), rolling them into balls with your hands. You should have about nineteen. Put the meatballs on a parchment-lined baking sheet (they release a lot of juices), and bake them until an instant-read thermometer inserted in the center of a meatball registers 155°F [68°C], 20 to 25 minutes. Transfer to a serving dish. Pour tomatillo salsa over and serve immediately.

This dish was inspired by my mom's leftover brisket. My dad loved brisket, and he'd bring home so much from the market that we always had leftovers, which I liked to eat cold. For Bar Amá, I wanted to make an appetizer that would be sort of like a brisket carpaccio—it's cooked but is almost as tender as raw meat and sliced very thinly. We use slow-roasted beef belly. To cut through the richness, sprinkle it with pomegranate seeds and give it a hit of lime juice.

SERVES 4 TO 6

About 3 lb [1.4 kg] beef deckle or brisket

2 Tbsp red-eye spice (page 36)

2 Tbsp pomegranate seeds

2 Tbsp finely grated cotija cheese

2 Tbsp radish, sliced into thin planks

1 Tbsp finely chopped red onion

1 Tbsp finely chopped fresh cilantro leaves

Pinch of flaky sea salt

Olive oil for drizzling

Juice of 1 or 2 limes

Rub the beef all over with the red-eye spice.

Heat the oven to 325°F [165°C]. Tightly wrap the beef with foil and put it on a rack on a foil-lined roasting pan. Add enough water to the pan so that it comes up the sides about ½ in [12 mm]. This helps prevent the fat drippings from burning on the bottom of the pan and adds a little moisture. Roast the beef until tender (it should be very soft to the touch), 4 to 5 hours. Add a little more water to the pan if it evaporates during cooking.

Cool the beef at room temperature for 30 minutes. Transfer to the refrigerator to cool completely (about 4 hours), so that it can be sliced thinly. When cool, heat the oven to 450°F [230°C].

Cut the beef against the grain into ⅛ in [4 mm] thick slices. You'll want three or four slices per person for an appetizer. (Any leftover beef is great for sandwiches, tacos, nachos, enchiladas, and even with eggs.) Put the slices on a baking sheet and warm in the oven until hot, 2 to 4 minutes.

Gently place the sliced beef on a platter and sprinkle with the pomegranate seeds, cotija, radish, onion, cilantro, and salt. Drizzle with olive oil, and then with lime juice. Serve immediately.

Everybody in my family remembers Amá's enchiladas—corn tortillas dipped in warm oil, rolled around queso fresco and finely diced raw onion, and garnished with a sofrito of carrot, potato, and still more onion. They were more like Mexican *tortillas enchiladas* than the cheese-covered enchilada platters served at restaurants. She would plate them one at a time and hand them to whoever was waiting to eat. Her tortillas were dyed red with annatto seed. I think red tortillas is a San Antonio thing, but nowadays they're often dyed with artificial coloring. Use plain corn tortillas, the best you can find.

SERVES 4

Carrot and potato sofrito

2 Tbsp olive oil

1 cup [115 g] finely chopped carrot (from 3 small peeled carrots)

*1 cup (175 g) finely chopped russet potato
(from 1 medium scrubbed, but not peeled, potato)*

⅔ cup [80 g] finely chopped onion (from 1 small onion)

2 garlic cloves, chopped

2 Tbsp finely chopped fresh cilantro leaves, plus more for garnish

¼ tsp fine sea salt

Fresh black pepper

Avocado or grapeseed oil for dipping tortillas

Eight 6 in [15 cm] corn tortillas

1½ cups [210 g] crumbled queso fresco

Chopped fresh cilantro leaves for garnish (optional)

MAKE THE SOFRITO: Heat the olive oil in a large skillet over medium-high heat until hot and shimmering. Add the carrot, potato, and onion. Reduce the heat to low and cook, stirring occasionally, until the vegetables are just tender, about 15 minutes.

Add the garlic, and cook until fragrant, about 1 minute (do not let it burn). Add the cilantro, salt, and a few grinds of pepper. Remove the sofrito from the heat and set aside.

Pour enough avocado oil into a skillet to cover the bottom and come up the sides slightly. When the oil is hot, using tongs, gently dip the tortillas in the oil, two at a time, to soften, about 5 seconds on each side. Transfer to a paper towel–lined plate as they are done. (Alternatively, wrap the tortillas in a kitchen towel and heat in the microwave until they are soft enough to roll easily, 1 to 2 minutes.)

Lay the tortillas flat on a work surface and fill each with 3 Tbsp queso fresco. Gently roll and put the enchiladas on a serving platter or individual plates. Garnish generously with the sofrito and cilantro, if desired. Serve immediately.

My brother and I played lacrosse in middle school and high school, and after practice we often ate my mom's green enchiladas. She'd make us a casserole each of tortillas rolled around chicken, cheese, and onions and smothered in tomatillo salsa and still more cheese, and serve them warm and bubbly, right out of the oven.

SERVES 4

2 to 3 cups [480 to 720 ml] tomatillo salsa (page 43)

1½ cups [210 g] crumbled queso fresco

1½ cups [200 g] shredded cooked chicken

3 Tbsp finely chopped onion

2 Tbsp finely chopped fresh cilantro leaves

Avocado or grapeseed oil for dipping tortillas

12 corn tortillas

½ cup [50 g] grated cheddar cheese

½ cup [50 g] grated Monterey Jack cheese

Heat the oven to 350°F [180°C].

Spread 2 to 3 Tbsp of the tomatillo salsa on the bottom of an 8 by 10 in [20 by 25 cm] baking dish (it should fit twelve filled and rolled tortillas snugly), and set aside.

Mix the queso fresco, chicken, onion, and cilantro in a medium bowl and set aside.

Pour enough oil into a skillet to cover the bottom and come up the sides slightly. Heat the oil over medium heat until hot. Using tongs, dip the tortillas in the hot oil, two at a time, to soften, about 5 seconds on each side. Transfer to a paper towel–lined plate as they are done. (Alternatively, wrap the tortillas in a kitchen towel and heat in the microwave until they are soft enough to roll easily, 1 to 2 minutes.)

In a small bowl, toss together the cheddar and Monterey Jack and set aside.

Set up your enchilada-making assembly line: First your warmed tortillas, next your queso fresco and chicken filling, and then your baking dish. Fill a tortilla with a generous 2 Tbsp of filling (be careful not to overstuff it). Tightly roll the tortilla around the filling and place, seam-side down, in the baking dish. Repeat until all of the enchiladas are rolled.

Spoon the tomatillo sauce over the top of the enchiladas, leaving the edges uncovered so that they get crispy. Top with the cheddar and Monterey Jack cheese mixture. Bake until the cheese is melted and bubbly, 15 to 20 minutes. Increase the heat to 400°F [200°C], and bake until the cheese is browned, about 5 minutes more. Remove from the oven, let the enchiladas rest for 5 minutes, and serve.

In Mexico, barbacoa is traditionally a whole animal slowly cooked over an open fire or in a hole in the ground lined with maguey leaves. (The word *barbecue* comes from *barbacoa*.) In Texas, it's usually a whole steer head steamed until tender, an adaptation introduced by Mexican ranchers. The Centeno Super Market had a to-go section in the butcher's department, and on weekends, it featured barbacoa—whole beef heads wrapped in foil and prepared in big steam cookers until the meat was tender enough to shred with a spoon. I make a variation of it with this *barbacoa cachete de res*, beef cheek braised with chiles and spices. If you plan to make beef cheek barbacoa enchiladas (page 97), don't throw out the braising liquid. You'll need it for the ranchero sauce.

SERVES 6 TO 8

2 guajillo chiles, stemmed and seeded

2 cascabel chiles, stemmed and seeded

4 cups [960 ml] water or beef broth, plus more as needed

About 3 lb [1.4 kg] beef cheeks

Fine sea salt and fresh ground pepper

¼ cup [60 ml] vegetable oil, plus more as needed

½ medium white onion, finely chopped, plus more for garnish

3 garlic cloves

1 Tbsp dried Mexican oregano, preferably Oregano Indio (see Note, page 17)

1 ½ tsp cumin seeds

2 whole cloves

½ tsp ground cinnamon

2 Tbsp apple cider vinegar

2 Tbsp dark brown sugar

Flour tortillas for serving, homemade (page 59) or store-bought, warmed in a skillet over medium heat

Your favorite hot sauce for serving

Finely chopped onion for garnish

Finely chopped fresh cilantro leaves for garnish

Heat the oven to 325°F [165°C].

Heat a dry skillet over medium-high heat. Add the chiles and toast them, stirring occasionally, so they start to release their oils, about 1 minute per side. Transfer to a small heat-proof bowl. In a small saucepan, bring 1 cup [240 ml] of the water to a boil and pour it over the chiles. Set aside.

Using a sharp knife, trim the silver skin and sinew from the beef cheeks. Cut the bigger cheeks in half so they're easier to sear. Sprinkle with salt and pepper.

Heat the oil in a large ovenproof pot with a lid, such as a Dutch oven, over medium-high heat until hot and shimmering. Sear the beef cheeks in batches, adding more oil if necessary, until nicely browned, 2 to 3 minutes on each side. Set aside.

Put the rehydrated chiles and their liquid in a blender, and add the onion, garlic, oregano, cumin seeds, cloves, cinnamon, vinegar, and brown sugar. Blend until puréed.

Add the chile purée to the pot of beef cheeks and add the remaining 3 cups [720 ml] water, or enough to cover the meat. Bring to a boil, and transfer the pot to the oven. Braise the beef until very tender (you should be able to shred it easily), about 2 hours.

Transfer the beef to a work surface. Reserve the braising liquid if you're making beef cheek barbacoa enchiladas (page 97). When the meat is cool enough to handle, shred into small chunks with a knife and fork. Serve with tortillas and hot sauce, and garnish with finely chopped onion and cilantro. Or use the shredded meat for the enchiladas. (You'll need about 3½ cups [375 g] shredded meat.) Store the meat and braising liquid in a covered container in the refrigerator for up to 2 days.

Tender, spicy, tomatoey beef cheek barbacoa, wrapped in a soft corn tortilla and baked with ranchero sauce and cheese until it's bubbly—that's a deluxe enchilada.

SERVES 4

Ranchero Sauce

Reserved braising liquid from beef cheek barbacoa (page 94)

One 14½ oz [412 g] can crushed San Marzano tomatoes

Avocado or grapeseed oil for dipping tortillas

Twelve 6 in [15 cm] corn tortillas

3½ cups [375 g] shredded meat from beef cheek barbacoa (page 94)

¾ cup [75 g] finely grated cheddar cheese

½ cup [70 g] crumbled queso fresco

3 Tbsp finely chopped white onion

Chopped fresh cilantro leaves for garnish

TO MAKE THE RANCHERO SAUCE: Pour all of the reserved barbacoa braising liquid into a blender, and add the crushed tomatoes. Blend to a smooth purée. Transfer to a small saucepan and simmer over medium heat, stirring occasionally, until reduced by about 1 cup [240 ml]. You should end up with about 3 cups [720 ml] of sauce.

Heat the oven to 400°F [200°C].

Grease the bottom and sides of an 8 by 10 in [20 by 25 cm] baking dish with butter or baking spray (it should fit twelve filled and rolled tortillas snugly). Spread 2 to 3 Tbsp of the ranchero sauce on the bottom of the dish and set aside.

Pour enough oil into a skillet to cover the bottom and come up the sides of the pan slightly. Heat the oil over medium heat until hot. Using tongs, dip the tortillas in the hot oil, two at a time, to soften, about 5 seconds on each side, adding more oil as needed. Transfer to a paper towel–lined plate as they are done. (Alternatively, wrap the tortillas in a kitchen towel and heat in the microwave until they are soft enough to roll easily, 1 to 2 minutes.)

Set up your enchilada-making assembly line: First your warmed tortillas, next your shredded barbacoa, grated cheddar cheese, and your baking dish. Fill a warm tortilla with a generous 2 Tbsp of shredded meat (be careful not to overstuff it). Sprinkle with a little bit of cheddar cheese. Roll tightly and place the enchilada, seam-side down, in the baking dish. Repeat until all of the enchiladas are rolled.

Spoon enough ranchero sauce to cover, and sprinkle queso fresco all over the tops of the enchiladas. Bake until the cheese is melted and bubbly, 15 to 20 minutes. Remove from the oven, sprinkle with onion and cilantro, and serve immediately.

Amá was the legendary cook in the family because she cooked simply and did so much with so little. She could make a delicious meal with a tomato, garlic, and some fideo. The word *fideo* refers to a thin noodle and to the Mexican and Tex-Mex dish it's used in. The dish is usually served as a soup, made with broth and tomatoes. Every Mexican family in Texas probably knows the Q and Q brand of fideo, sold in bright yellow boxes with red lettering. As soon as I saw the box on the counter, I knew what was for dinner. At Bar Amá, fideo is the base—somewhere between soup and a pasta dish—for one of the restaurant's best sellers: fideo with octopus (page 99). But you can also serve this recipe on its own as a vegetarian side dish.

SERVES 4

2 Tbsp avocado oil

One 5 oz [140 g] package fideo pasta

¼ medium white onion, finely chopped

1 garlic clove, finely chopped

½ tsp fine sea salt, plus more for seasoning

⅛ tsp cumin seeds

1 tsp Amá spice mix (page 32) or chile powder

½ cup [120 ml] low-sodium V8 vegetable juice

1½ cups [360 ml] vegetable broth or water

1 Tbsp Mexican sriracha (page 29)

1 lime

Fresh black pepper

Heat the avocado oil in a sauté pan or large saucepan over high heat until hot and shimmering. Add the fideo and fry until browned, 2 to 3 minutes.

Add the onion and garlic, give a stir, and cook for 1 minute. Add the salt, cumin seeds, and spice mix and stir to combine. Add the V8 and 1 cup [240 ml] of the broth and bring to a boil over medium-high heat. Cook, stirring occasionally, until nearly all of the liquid has been absorbed.

Stir in the remaining ½ cup [120 ml] of broth and the Mexican sriracha. Cover, lower the heat to medium, and cook until the fideo is tender and the sauce has thickened, 5 to 10 minutes. Adjust the salt to taste. Juice the lime over the fideo and top with a few grinds of black pepper. Serve immediately, or set aside for the fideo with octopus recipe (page 99).

Tomatoes and garlic go so well with octopus that it seemed like a natural match for fideo (page 98), garnished with crunchy pepitas and radishes. Fideo, like paella, is a base for all kinds of ingredients, including sautéed chunks of chicken breast, braised short rib, sausages, shrimp, or vegetables. Sometimes we add sliced sautéed kielbasa to this, too.

NOTE : Ask your fishmonger for cleaned octopus with the tentacles separated, or ask for the octopus tentacles only.

SERVES 4

1 small bunch fresh cilantro

2 lb [910 grams] octopus tentacles

Fine sea salt

4 cups [960 ml] water

1 cup [240 ml] Mexican beer

1 cup [240 ml] apple cider vinegar

1 carrot, cut into chunks

½ celery stalk

1 onion, halved crosswise

1 tsp chile powder

½ tsp coriander seeds

½ tsp fennel seeds

½ tsp caraway seeds

½ tsp black peppercorns

½ tsp dried Mexican oregano, preferably Oregano Indio (see Note, page 17)

1 Tbsp avocado or olive oil

1 recipe fideo (page 98)

3 Tbsp sliced green onions (green part only) for garnish

3 Tbsp radishes, sliced into thin planks for garnish

2 Tbsp toasted pepitas or 1 tsp toasted sesame seeds for garnish

Chop a few cilantro leaves and set aside for a garnish. Put the octopus tentacles in a large bowl and rub with 1 Tbsp salt. Set aside while you prepare the cooking broth.

Pour the water, beer, and vinegar into a large pot over medium heat, and add the carrot, celery, onion, and the remaining cilantro. Add the chile powder, coriander seeds, fennel seeds, caraway seeds, peppercorns, and oregano. Bring to a simmer.

Rinse the octopus and add it to the simmering broth. Simmer, partially covered, turning the octopus occasionally, until it is tender enough to cut with a spoon, about 40 minutes.

CONT'D

FIDEO

nicelli

MACARRONES ENRIQUECIDOS

NET WT./PESO NETO 5 OZ.(142g)

BRAND ®

ORIGINAL

verm

ENRICHED MACARONI / MAC

THE ORIGINAL FIDEO
SINCE 1910

2

Quality

Quantity

FIDEO

nicelli

MACARRONES ENRIQUECIDOS

NET WT./PESO NETO 5 OZ.(142g)

2 AND 2

BRAND ®

ORIGINAL

verm

ENRICHED MACARONI / MAC

EASY
OPENER

THE ORIGINAL
FIDEO SINCE
1910

Quality

Quantity

FIDEO

nicelli

2 AND 2

BRAND ®

ORIGINAL

verm

Fill a medium bowl halfway with ice and add some of the cooking liquid. Carefully transfer the octopus tentacles to the bowl, so that they don't fall apart. Let cool. Transfer to a paper towel–lined plate and refrigerate for 30 minutes to 1 hour so that they dry completely and continue to cool.

Using a sharp knife held at an angle, cut each of the tentacles on the bias into four equal pieces. Heat the oil in a large skillet over medium-high heat until hot and shimmering. Sear the octopus pieces until the edges are well browned, 2 to 3 minutes on each side.

Add the finished fideo and cook, stirring, until warmed through. Transfer to a platter and garnish with the green onion, radish, reserved chopped cilantro, and pepitas.

The Gulf Coast is known for its shrimp, and when I was growing up, Port Aransas, Texas, about 180 mi [290 km] southeast of San Antonio, had some of the best. On the occasional road trip to the coast, we would eat baked redfish and shrimp ceviche (with a ton of Big Red soda). The key to good shrimp ceviche is simple: You need to have the freshest shrimp, otherwise don't bother. This recipe has been adapted over the years. At Bar Amá, we make the ceviche with grapefruit, and serve it with avocado and fresh, crunchy tortilla chips for scooping it up.

SERVES 4

Grated zest of ½ grapefruit, plus 1 cup [240 ml] fresh grapefruit juice (from about 2 grapefruits)

1 lb [455 g] Gulf shrimp (16/25 count) or any fresh shrimp, peeled and deveined

2 shallots, cut crosswise into thin rings

2 serrano chiles, stemmed, cut into thin rings, and seeded

1 garlic clove, thinly sliced

Grated zest of 1 lime, plus ½ cup [120 ml] fresh lime juice (from about 5 limes)

Grated zest of 2 lemons, plus ½ cup [120 ml] fresh lemon juice (from 3 lemons)

½ cup [120 ml] distilled white vinegar

1 bunch watercress, leaves and thin stems only

2 Tbsp extra-virgin olive oil

1 avocado, pitted, peeled, and cut into a large dice

Fine sea salt and fresh black pepper

¼ tsp Amá spice mix (page 32) or chile powder, for garnish

3 radishes, thinly sliced, for garnish

Tortilla chips (page 187) for serving

Your favorite hot sauce for serving

Pour the grapefruit juice into a small saucepan, bring to a boil over high heat, and continue boiling until the juice is reduced to about ¼ cup [60 ml] and is slightly syrupy, about 10 minutes.

Cut the shrimp into bite-size chunks and put them in a medium bowl or container. Add the shallots, serranos, and garlic.

In another medium bowl, stir together the reduced grapefruit juice and zest, lime juice and zest, lemon juice and zest, and vinegar. Pour the mixture over the shrimp and marinate for at least 1 hour and up to 6 hours (depending on how "cooked" you want your ceviche).

Drain the shrimp, discarding the liquid, and transfer to a medium bowl. Stir in the watercress, olive oil, and avocado, and season with salt and pepper. Garnish with the spice mix and radishes. Transfer to a platter and serve with tortilla chips and hot sauce.

SCALLOP AGUACHILE WITH TOMATO-HABANERO WATER AND GOOSEBERRIES

Aguachile is a ceviche traditionally made in the Mexican state of Sinaloa with fresh raw shrimp, cucumber, red onion, lime juice, and chiles. It isn't exactly a Tex-Mex dish, but my family made a version of it: We would take the liquid from a bowl of pico de gallo and pour it over raw shrimp. At Bar Amá, we make with it with scallops during tomato season. The kitchen makes tomato water from fresh tomatoes and habanero chiles and pours that and lime juice over raw scallops, pickled gooseberries, cucumbers, and shallots. Aguachile is traditionally served immediately, without marinating. But if you want the acid in the lime juice and vinegar to slightly "cook" the seafood, you can marinate it for a bit. A great summer dish to enjoy with a cold beer and a wedge of lime.

SERVES 4 TO 6

Tomato-habanero water

1 lb (455 g) cherry tomatoes

1 shallot, chopped

1 large garlic clove

1 habanero chile, stemmed and seeded

½ cup [8 g] fresh cilantro leaves

10 fresh basil leaves

3 Tbsp pineapple vinegar (see Note, page 107) or distilled white vinegar

1 Tbsp fine sea salt

12 oz [340 g] sea scallops (about 12), side muscle removed

2 Tbsp fresh lime juice

½ lemon cucumber, thinly sliced

12 pickled gooseberries (page 27), halved

1 shallot, thinly sliced into rings

1 serrano or jalapeño chile, stemmed, thinly sliced into rings, and seeded

Finely chopped fresh cilantro leaves for garnish

Extra-virgin olive oil for drizzling

Flaky sea salt and fresh black pepper

Line a fine-mesh sieve with cheesecloth and set it over a large bowl.

MAKE THE TOMATO-HABANERO WATER: Combine the tomatoes, shallot, garlic, habanero, cilantro, basil, vinegar, and fine sea salt in a food processor and pulse until coarsely chopped. Transfer the mixture to the prepared sieve. Cover and refrigerate for at least 2 hours and up to 4. (Do not stir or press on the solids, or the tomato water will be cloudy.) Discard the solids, cover the tomato water, and refrigerate until ready to use.

CONT'D

Cut each scallop crosswise into thirds, so that you have three thin, round slices.

Put the scallops in a medium bowl and pour over the lime juice and tomato water. Serve immediately, or if you wish, marinate the scallops for 1 to 3 hours in the refrigerator.

To serve, divide the scallops and the juice and tomato water among four to six shallow bowls. Add the cucumber, and arrange the scallop and cucumber slices attractively. Top with the pickled gooseberry halves, shallot, and chile. Garnish with cilantro leaves and a drizzle of olive oil. Season with flaky sea salt and a grind of fresh black pepper and serve.

Sayulita, Mexico. The bus dropped us off at the ocean, and a guy named Chavo took us on a boat to a secret surf break. Skipjack were flying out of the water. After we surfed, we were looking for somewhere to eat. Somebody had set up a giant grill on the sand to cook the first *huachinango* (red snapper). We each got a whole roasted fish, drank Coronas, and sat on the beach. This is the fish that reminds me of that beach, drizzled all over with a punchy, herbaceous sauce.

NOTE : Pineapple and banana vinegars are available at some gourmet shops and online, such as at the Rancho Gordo website.

SERVES 4

Tex-Mex chimichurri

½ cup [120 ml] pineapple or banana vinegar

1 tsp fine sea salt, plus more for seasoning

1 garlic clove, thinly sliced or minced

1 shallot, finely chopped

*3 fresh pequín chiles, or ½ fresh arbol chile,
stemmed, seeded, and finely chopped*

½ cup [14 g] finely chopped fresh cilantro leaves

*1 tsp dried Mexican oregano, preferably Oregano Indio
(see Note, page 17), or 1 Tbsp fresh Mexican oregano*

½ cup [120 ml] extra-virgin olive oil

Juice of 2 limes

Two 1½ lb [680 g] whole sea bream, cleaned and descaled

1 Tbsp fine sea salt

2 tsp fresh black pepper

4 sprigs fresh thyme

2 dried bay leaves

1 lime, cut into 8 slices

2 Tbsp olive oil

MAKE THE CHIMICHURRI: Mix together the vinegar, salt, garlic, shallot, and chiles in a medium bowl and let stand for 10 minutes. Stir in the cilantro and oregano. Using a fork, whisk in the oil and lime juice. Taste and add more salt if desired.

Heat the oven to 400°F [200°C].

Sprinkle each fish all over, inside and out, with 1½ tsp salt and 1 tsp black pepper. Stuff the cavity of each fish with 2 sprigs thyme, a bay leaf, and 4 slices of lime.

CONT'D

107

Heat a large cast-iron or other heavy-bottom skillet over high heat. Rub each fish all over with the olive oil. When the pan is very hot, sear one of the fish on both sides until well browned, 2 to 3 minutes per side. Transfer to a baking sheet. Repeat with the second fish.

Roast the fish until the meat under the gills and belly is completely opaque. Or gently pull the meat nearest the tail; it should pull away from the bone easily. Remove from the oven and transfer to a platter. Drizzle the chimichurri over the fish and serve immediately.

This is a holiday dish at Bar Amá, a Tex-Mex version of Auguste Escoffier's classic lobster Thermidor made with crema, hot sauce, tortilla chips, and cheddar and Monterey Jack cheeses. Mixed with the lobster meat, the whole thing is cooked in the cleaned shell and topped with still more gooey melted cheese. Serve with tortillas and a bottle of cold Chablis.

SERVES 4

Two 2 ¼ lb [1 kg] lobsters

1 Tbsp olive oil

1 garlic clove, minced

1 cup [100 g] finely grated cheddar cheese

1 cup [100 g] finely grated Monterey Jack cheese

2 ½ Tbsp morita-guajillo salsa (page 31) or your favorite hot sauce

2 Tbsp crema Mexicana or sour cream

½ tsp fine sea salt

8 tortilla chips, coarsely crushed by hand

2 Tbsp chopped fresh chives for garnish

Prepare an ice bath by filling a large stainless steel bowl with ice water and set aside. Bring a large pot of water to a rolling boil. Add both lobsters and cover. Boil the lobsters for 9 minutes.

Transfer them to the ice bath to cool, about 5 minutes.

Heat the oven to 450°F [230°C].

Heat the olive oil in a small skillet over medium heat. Add the garlic and cook until golden, about 1 minute. Remove from the heat and set that aside while you prepare the lobsters.

Using kitchen shears, split the lobster shells in half lengthwise, starting from the tail. Remove the tail meat and set aside.

For Maine lobsters, use kitchen shears to halve the claws as well (spiny lobsters don't have claws). With the kitchen shears, remove the top half of the claw shell, cutting along the crease of the claw (it's kind of like opening the lid of a box). Remove the claw meat and set aside with the tail meat.

Discard the remaining lobster innards. Rinse and dry the shells, including the claws, if using Maine lobsters, and put them on a baking sheet.

Cut the lobster meat into roughly ½ in [12 mm] chunks and transfer to a large bowl. In a medium bowl, combine the two cheeses. In a small bowl, whisk together the salsa and crema, and fold the mixture into the lobster meat. Add the reserved garlic, salt, half the cheese mixture, and the tortilla chips.

Fill the lobster shells (and the claws, too, if using Maine lobsters), sprinkle with the remaining cheese, and put the baking sheet in the oven. Bake the lobsters until the cheese is melted and bubbly, about 5 minutes.

Remove from the oven and transfer the lobster to a platter. Sprinkle with the chives and serve immediately.

THEY MET AT OLMOS PHARMACY

I think Nana and Grandpa, my maternal grand-parents, were the ultimate Tex-Mex couple. Maria de la Luz Martinez (everyone called her Luz) was a Mexican-American teenager from San Antonio's West Side when she met William McMunn Jr., a chino-wearing German-Irish kid living in Jefferson Heights, around 1950. They fell in love at Olmos Pharmacy, a landmark Art Deco soda fountain where a lot of teenagers shared milkshakes.

But most of the other couples who met at Olmos Pharmacy in the '50s weren't interracial, and Nana and Grandpa faced disapproval and discrimination, even from their own families.

Nana, who might have been considered worldly for venturing into the Olmos Park–Monte Vista neighborhood to get a job, worked at the soda fountain. Nana's father, my Apá, drove her to each of her shifts at the pharmacy in his blue pickup truck, which he used to haul produce for his vegetable stand at El Mercado. She would tell him that someday she was going to live in this ritzy neighborhood of turn-of-the-century mansions and charming stone cottages. He would smile and say, "*Si, mi hija*" ("Yes, my daughter").

Olmos Pharmacy employees were allowed to eat anything at the counter except the steaks, because those were for the customers. So when Nana felt like having steak, she would go to the nearby Handy Andy grocery store and buy her own, and the cook, Jesse, would grill it for her. Nana had a way of getting what she wanted.

When Grandpa walked into Olmos Pharmacy for lunch one day, Nana was there taking orders. Their eyes met, and Grandpa became a regular at the counter. He didn't strike up conversations with Nana, and he didn't immediately ask her out. For fun, Nana started chatting him up in Spanish so that he wouldn't understand what she was saying, talking about how all the girls must like him: "*Eres muy guapo.*" ("You are so handsome.") He would continue to eat his lunch and smile at her without saying anything.

After a while he started taking his coffee breaks there too. He was working at his father's marble and stone company at the time, and my great-grandfather, William Sr. ("Mac"), wondered what was up. Still, Grandpa hadn't asked Nana out or even had a real conversation with her. He'd just listen to her say her little nothings in Spanish while he ate his lunch or drank his coffee.

Finally, after weeks, he asked her out for a date. To Nana's shock and embarrassment, he asked her out in fluent Spanish. He had understood everything she had said all along.

They started going out to the movies, mostly in secret, because Apá didn't want his daughter going out with a gringo. Apá once pulled out a .38 and shot at the car Grandpa borrowed from his friend Buddy to pick up Nana for a date. (Grandpa had to borrow wheels because he rode a motorcycle.) Apá chased him as soon as he got out of the car, and Grandpa ran, leaving it behind (Buddy picked it up later and drove off real fast). Meanwhile, Amá cried because she was afraid Nana would be mistreated by Grandpa, his family, and others who might ridicule or harass them. And though Great-Granddad Mac always liked Nana, Grandpa's mother, Great-Grandma Haddie, was icy toward her.

Grandpa might have been a gringo, but his family on both sides had moved from Ireland and Germany, respectively, to settle in northern Mexico. Like Amá and Apá, they were driven out by the Mexican Revolution. Grandpa was hip, and he took Nana dancing at the West Side's Keyhole Club, a jazz and swing club that was "black and tan"—racially tolerant at a time when segregation was still common. Nat King Cole played there, and so did Dizzy Gillespie—for a black, white, and Mexican crowd. (The club was instrumental in the development of the West Side sound — Tejano rhythm and blues.) When a new police commissioner tried to shut it down in the early '50s, the owner went to court to keep it open. He won, an early civil rights victory in San Antonio.

Maybe that was a cue. Finally, Great-Granddad Mac went to talk to Apá directly, and he spoke to him in perfect Spanish. Apá gave the couple his blessing to marry, and eventually even Great-Grandma Haddie came around.

Ultimately, Grandpa and Nana were both Texan and both Mexican, one was white and the other brown. They were a couple from multiple cultures who were also deeply rooted in San Antonio. That's more Tex-Mex than the Tex-Mex of salt-rimmed margaritas, sizzling platters, and bowls of queso.

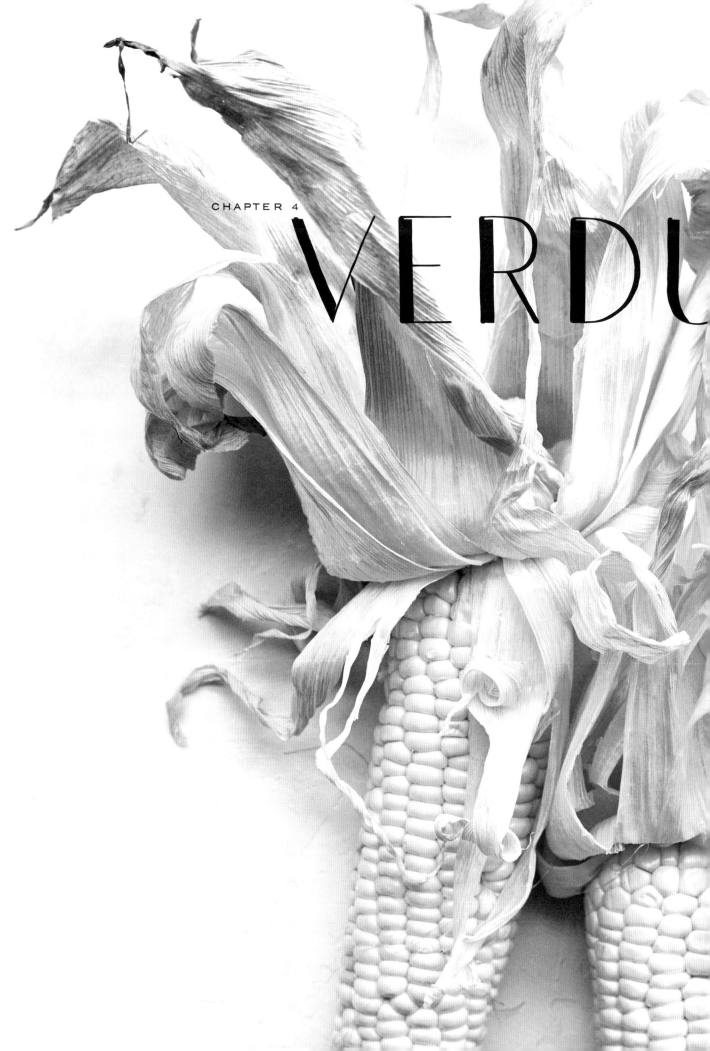

CHAPTER 4

VERDU

RAS

EL TOMATE

Escarole is one of my favorite leafy green vegetables, a chicory that's slightly bitter but pleasant. It goes great with salty cheeses, briny olives, punchy radishes, and aromatic herbs. In a salad, it's a canvas that doesn't fade into the background but doesn't overwhelm other ingredients, either. At Bar Amá, we add a lot of what's fresh from the markets, maybe shaved carrots and radishes, along with Beldi olives, baked cotija (for its caramelized flavor), and sometimes finely grated bottarga. We'll make a fruity vinegar with bananas or *plantanos* (plantains), which are really good in salad dressings (also awesome in ceviches and for pickling vegetables).

SERVES 4

Baked cotija
One 8 oz [225 g] chunk cotija cheese

Cotija croutons
Heaping 4 cups [210 g] cubed bread
2 garlic cloves, minced
2 tsp fresh thyme leaves
¼ tsp fine sea salt
⅓ cup [80 ml] extra-virgin olive oil
1½ Tbsp finely grated cotija cheese

Banana vinaigrette
⅓ cup [80 ml] banana vinegar (see Note, page 107)
Juice of 1 lime
½ tsp Dijon mustard
Pinch of fine sea salt
Fresh black pepper
½ cup [120 ml] extra-virgin olive oil

2 heads escarole, trimmed and cut crosswise into ribbons
1 small carrot, peeled and thinly shaved on a mandoline
2 watermelon radishes, thinly shaved on a mandoline
10 cherry tomatoes, halved
10 Beldi or other dry-cured black olives, pitted and halved
1 Tbsp finely grated bottarga (optional)

MAKE THE BAKED COTIJA: Heat the oven to 350°F [180°C]. Put the chunk of cotija in a baking dish and bake until toasted brown on the outside, 15 to 20 minutes. Remove from the oven and let cool. Finely grate the cooled cotija and set aside.

117

CONT'D

Increase the oven temperature to 375°F [190 °C].

MAKE THE CROUTONS: In a large bowl, combine the bread, garlic, thyme, and salt. Drizzle the olive oil over the bread, stirring constantly, and continue stirring until the bread is coated with the seasonings and the olive oil is absorbed.

Spread out the bread cubes in an even layer on a baking sheet. Don't crowd the pan. Bake until golden brown and crisp, about 10 minutes. If you're using super fresh bread, it'll take a little longer, and if the bread is stale and dry, it may brown faster. As soon as it comes out of the oven, sprinkle the finely grated fresh cotija on top and set aside.

MAKE THE VINAIGRETTE: In a jar with a tight-fitting lid, combine the banana vinegar, lime juice, mustard, salt, and a few grinds of pepper. Shake well to combine. Add the olive oil, shake again, and set aside.

To assemble the salad, combine the escarole, carrot, radishes, tomatoes, olives, and 2 Tbsp of the grated baked cotija in a large salad bowl.

Pour ½ cup [120 ml] of the dressing over the salad and toss. (Add more dressing, if desired.) Garnish with the croutons, the remaining grated baked cotija, and the bottarga, if using. Serve immediately.

I love Caesar salad and make a version of it at each of my restaurants, including this one at Bar Amá. This is a Tex-Mex version with chile spice and cotija cheese on the croutons and in the dressing. There's more cotija on top of the salad, too, along with avocado. And, of course, it wouldn't be a Caesar salad without garlic, anchovies, and mayo.

SERVES 4

Croutons

3 Tbsp extra-virgin olive oil

1 garlic clove

1 Tbsp fresh thyme leaves

1 Tbsp chopped fresh oregano

1 Tbsp Amá spice mix (page 32) or chile powder

Pinch of fine sea salt

Fresh black pepper

3 cups [155 g] bite-size pieces of torn sourdough bread

2 Tbsp finely grated cotija cheese

Dressing

¼ cup [60 ml] extra-virgin olive oil

4 to 6 anchovy fillets, drained and finely chopped, plus more whole anchovies for garnish (optional)

3 garlic cloves, finely chopped

½ tsp Amá spice mix (page 32) or chile powder

¼ cup [60 g] mayonnaise

Zest and juice of 1 lime, plus more as needed

1 Tbsp Dijon mustard

2 tsp Worcestershire sauce

2 Tbsp coarsely chopped fresh cilantro leaves

½ tsp fine sea salt

½ tsp fresh black pepper, plus more for seasoning

1 or 2 Tbsp finely grated cotija cheese

2 large romaine hearts, coarsely chopped

1 ripe avocado, pitted, peeled, and diced

½ cup [50 g] grated cotija cheese or Parmigiano-Reggiano

½ cup [70 g] crumbled queso fresco

119

CONT'D

Heat the oven to 375°F [190°C].

MAKE THE CROUTONS: Whisk together the olive oil, garlic, thyme, oregano, spice mix, salt, and a few grinds of black pepper. Put the torn bread pieces on a baking sheet and drizzle with the oil mixture, tossing to coat evenly. Sprinkle the cheese on top and toss to incorporate. Bake until golden and crisp, 10 to 15 minutes.

MAKE THE DRESSING: Pour the olive oil into a small skillet and add the anchovies, garlic, and spice mix. Heat over medium-low heat, stirring, until the anchovies begin to break down, 1 to 2 minutes. Set aside to cool. In a medium bowl, combine the mayonnaise, lime zest and juice, mustard, Worcestershire sauce, cilantro, salt, and pepper. Whisk in the cooled oil with anchovies and garlic. Taste to adjust the pepper and lime, if needed. Add the cotija cheese, and set aside.

To assemble the salad, put the romaine, croutons, avocado, and cotija cheese in a large bowl and toss to coat with the dressing. Sprinkle the crumbled queso fresco on top, scatter a few anchovy fillets on top, if desired, and serve immediately.

This is a salad dedicated to two of my cooks, the Vasquez brothers from Oaxaca, who used to make fun of me when I brought in cases of watercress or arugula, saying, "Hey, Pa, this is food for goats. You have a goat?" Watercress, related to mustard greens and horseradish, is a little peppery and awakens the senses. I like a great salad to balance the cheesiness of Tex-Mex, but the greens have to hold up to a lot of flavor. Watercress does that; it's good with fatty foods. This is a midsummer salad, when stone fruit and tomatoes are at peak ripeness.

SERVES 4

4 bunches watercress, fibrous stems removed

2 nectarines, pitted and cut into 8 wedges

1 large heirloom tomato, cut into 8 wedges

¼ cup [25 g] grated Mahón cheese, plus extra for garnish

Creamy lime dressing

2 Tbsp heavy cream

1 Tbsp lime juice, plus lime zest for garnish

1 tsp toasted sesame seeds

Fine sea salt

Fresh black pepper

¼ cup [60 ml] extra-virgin olive oil

Toss the watercress, nectarines, tomato, and cheese in a large salad bowl and set aside.

MAKE THE DRESSING: In a jar with a tight-fitting lid, combine the cream, lime juice, sesame seeds, a pinch of salt, and a few grinds of black pepper. Shake well to combine. Add the olive oil and shake again. Adjust the seasoning to taste.

To assemble the salad, pour the dressing over the salad and toss to combine. Garnish with a little extra cheese and lime zest and serve immediately.

This broccolini torrada is one of the original Bar Amá dishes and will always be on the menu. *Torrada* means "toasted," a reference to the toasted nuts in this Mexican-inspired version of bagna cauda, an Italian condiment of warmed olive oil with anchovies and garlic. Our torrada is heavy on the toasted nuts and anchovies, with a little bit of cilantro, tepin chiles (they have a kick), and cumin. I really like rich, nutty, salty torrada with the slightly bitter broccolini.

SERVES 4 TO 6

Torrada

2 Tbsp coarsely chopped pecans

2 Tbsp coarsely chopped walnuts

1 garlic clove

4 anchovy fillets, chopped

2 Tbsp finely chopped cilantro

2 Tbsp olive oil

Zest and juice of ½ lime

3 dried tepin or arbol chiles (or more if you want it hotter)

⅛ tsp ground coriander

⅛ tsp ground cumin

Pinch of fine sea salt

Fresh black pepper

3 bunches broccolini

1 Tbsp olive oil

Pinch of fine sea salt

Fresh black pepper

3 Tbsp finely grated aged white cheddar cheese

Mexican sriracha (page 29) for garnish

Thinly sliced radish for garnish (optional)

MAKE THE TORRADA: Toast the nuts and whole garlic clove in a small, dry skillet until lightly browned and fragrant, 2 to 3 minutes. Put the nuts in a large bowl. Finely chop the toasted garlic and add it to the bowl. Mix in the anchovies, cilantro, olive oil, lime zest and juice, chiles, coriander, and cumin. Season with the salt and 2 grinds of black pepper. Set aside.

Heat the broiler. Put the broccolini on a baking sheet and toss with the olive oil. Season with the salt and a few grinds of black pepper. Broil until just tender and the edges are browned, about 10 minutes, tossing once halfway through cooking.

Toss the broccolini with the torrada and transfer to a platter. Sprinkle with the cheddar and garnish with the Mexican sriracha and radish, if using. Serve immediately.

This was inspired by my mom's steamed cauliflower, which she would serve as a side with pasta with pesto sauce. She made the pesto with whatever nuts were on hand, and it being Texas, that was often pecans. I riffed on her variation by using cilantro instead of basil and cotija instead of Parmigiano-Reggiano. Like the broccolini torrada (page 125), this is always on the menu at Bar Amá.

SERVES 4

NOTE : Blanching the cilantro for the pesto helps prevent it from oxidizing.

Cilantro-pecan pesto

2 bunches fresh cilantro (leaves and soft stems only)

½ cup [65 g] toasted pecans or cashews

3 Tbsp grated cotija cheese

Zest of 2 lemons

1 garlic clove

¼ to ⅓ cup [60 to 80 ml] olive oil

1 head cauliflower, florets separated

3 Tbsp olive oil

Pinch of fine sea salt

Fresh black pepper

2 fresh thyme sprigs (optional—if you have some around, great)

⅓ cup [35 g] grated cotija cheese

Juice of 1 lime

MAKE THE PESTO: Prepare an ice bath by filling a large bowl with ice water; set aside. Bring a medium pot of water to a boil. Add the cilantro and cook just until bright green, 1 minute. Transfer to the ice bath to stop the cooking and drain. Squeeze out as much excess moisture as possible with your hands or in a clean kitchen towel. Coarsely chop the cilantro and put it in a food processor. Add the nuts, cheese, lemon zest, and garlic. Pulse until a coarse purée forms (it should be fairly chunky). Drizzle in the olive oil and pulse until it's the desired consistency. Set aside.

Heat the broiler. Put the cauliflower florets on a baking sheet and toss with the olive oil. Season with the salt, a few grinds of black pepper, and the thyme, if using. Broil until the cauliflower is just tender and the edges are well browned, about 10 minutes, tossing once halfway through cooking.

Remove the cauliflower from the oven and toss with about ½ cup [120 ml] of the cilantro-pecan pesto. (Reserve any extra pesto for another use; store, covered, in the refrigerator for up to 2 days.) Transfer the cauliflower to a serving plate. Sprinkle with the cotija and then the lime juice, and serve immediately.

These Brussels sprouts are so easy to make. Quartered so that they cook faster, they're broiled until tender and charred. Then they're tossed with tomatoey Mexican salmorejo, pickled onions, and mint. I really like that combination of ingredients—with good acidity from the tomatoes and pickled onions and freshness from the mint.

SERVES 4

Generous 1 lb [470 g] Brussels sprouts, quartered

2 Tbsp olive oil

Pinch of fine sea salt

Fresh black pepper

⅓ cup [80 ml] Mexican salmorejo (page 28)

¼ cup [55 g] pickled oregano onions (page 25)

4 or 5 large fresh mint leaves, torn

Queso fresco for garnish (optional)

Position a rack in the lower half of the oven and heat the broiler.

Put the Brussels sprouts on a baking sheet and toss with olive oil, salt, and a few grinds of pepper. Broil until cooked through and charred at the edges, 8 to 10 minutes, flipping the Brussels sprouts halfway through cooking.

Transfer the Brussels sprouts to a bowl and toss with the salmorejo, pickled onions, and torn mint. Garnish with queso fresco, if desired, and serve immediately.

My introduction to Mexican street corn was outside of the first Centeno Super Market, where there was always someone with a cart selling corn smeared with butter and dusted with chile powder. I moved on to next-level corn at the local rodeos, which would be mixed with mayo, bacon, breadcrumbs of some sort, and lime. I like it with a sprinkling of cotija cheese. Nothing hits the spot like corn and fat together.

SERVES 4

3 slices bacon

Kernels cut from 4 ears corn

5 oz [140 g] hen of the wood mushrooms, broken apart

1 garlic clove

1 Tbsp finely chopped shallot

1 serrano chile, stemmed, seeded, and thinly sliced

1 Tbsp chopped fresh cilantro

10 fresh mint leaves, torn

1 Tbsp mayonnaise

3 Tbsp grated cotija cheese

Cook the bacon in a large skillet over medium heat until the edges are browned and the fat rendered, about 10 minutes.

Add the corn and mushrooms, raise the heat to medium-high, and sauté until the vegetables are cooked through and their edges are caramelized, 2 to 3 minutes. Add the garlic, shallot, and chile and cook until aromatic but not browned, 1 minute.

Remove from the heat and stir in the cilantro, mint, mayonnaise, and cotija. Serve warm, or chilled as a salad. If not using right away, store in a covered container in the refrigerator for up to 1 day.

I like red kuri, kabocha, and other squashes and pumpkins with a low moisture content, because once cooked, they still have a firm, toothsome bite. Calabaza (or fairy-tale) pumpkins work well, too. I roast them with butter and a little bit of chile and piloncillo or turbinado sugar, so they're also fragrant. Their earthy, subtle sweetness is delicious with the nutty butter and spicy chile. A great side dish or the centerpiece of a vegetarian meal.

SERVES 8

2 red kuri squashes, or 1 large kabocha or other Asian squash

2 tsp fine sea salt

½ cup [110 g] unsalted butter

4 tsp grated piloncillo (see Note, page 58) or turbinado sugar

1 pasilla de Oaxaca chile, stemmed, seeded, and torn into 4 pieces

4 sprigs fresh thyme

4 Tbsp water

Heat the oven to 350°F [180°C].

Cut the stems off of the kuri squashes and discard. Cut each squash in half lengthwise (starting from the stem end). Scoop out and discard the seeds. Put the squash halves on a baking sheet, cavity-side up. Sprinkle ½ tsp salt over each of the halves. Into the cavity of each half, add 2 Tbsp butter, 1 tsp piloncillo, a piece of the pasilla chile, a sprig of thyme, and 1 Tbsp water. Cover each half with foil. Bake until the squash is very tender, about 1 hour. Cut each half into four pieces, transfer to a platter, and serve immediately.

I think pimento cheese is such a good filling for vegetables—peppers, chiles, and especially squash blossoms. They're beautiful and always delicious battered and fried. They remind me of the fritto misto at one of the seafood shacks we'd visit on summer trips to the Gulf Coast. They also say "summer in California."

SERVES 4 TO 6

Lace batter

¾ cup [105 g] cornstarch

½ cup [70 g] all-purpose flour

¼ tsp baking soda

Pinch of fine sea salt

1¼ to 1½ cups [300 to 360 ml] club soda

2½ cups [570 g] cascabel pimento cheese (page 47)

12 zucchini blossoms, stamens removed

Vegetable oil (such as avocado or grapeseed) or peanut oil for frying

Flaky sea salt

Lime wedges for serving

MAKE THE LACE BATTER: Whisk together the cornstarch, flour, baking soda, and fine sea salt in a medium bowl until well combined. Whisk in enough of the club soda so the batter is liquidy, but will coat the back of a spoon (when you run your finger across the back of the spoon, there should be a clean trail). Refrigerate while you fill the squash blossoms.

Scoop the pimento cheese into a piping bag, cut a small opening at the tip, and fill each blossom. Refrigerate until firm, about 1 hour.

In a large pot, heat about 2 in [5 cm] of oil over medium-high heat until a deep-fry thermometer registers 350°F [180°C].

Dredge a filled squash blossom in the lace batter, shaking off the excess. Gently lay it in the oil to fry. Fry a few at a time, without crowding the pan, dredging each blossom right before it goes into the oil. Cook, flipping once with a slotted spoon, until golden brown, 2 to 3 minutes total. Transfer to paper towels to drain. Repeat until all of the blossoms are fried. Sprinkle with flaky sea salt and serve immediately with lime wedges.

I'm a fan of California persimmons, which arrive in the fall. There always seems to be an explosion of them at the markets and on neighborhood trees. I've put them in salads and baked goods and used them for preserves. Here they're sautéed in butter and sprinkled with lime juice, for an easy side dish for roast meats, or to enjoy with other small plates as part of a vegetarian meal. A little more crema might even nudge it toward dessert.

SERVES 4

1½ Tbsp unsalted butter

3 Fuyu persimmons, quartered

Pinch of fine sea salt

Fresh black pepper

Juice of ½ lime

2 or 3 Tbsp crema Mexicana or crème fraîche

Flaky sea salt

Several fresh mint leaves, torn

1½ tsp extra-virgin olive oil

Heat a large skillet over medium heat, add the butter, and increase the heat to high. When the butter starts to sizzle and brown, add the persimmons and sauté until well browned at the edges, about 4 minutes. Season with fine sea salt and a few grinds of pepper, and transfer to paper towels to drain.

Transfer the persimmons to a serving plate and sprinkle with the lime juice. Dollop with crema. Garnish with a sprinkle of flaky sea salt, mint, and olive oil. Serve immediately.

This easy dish of roasted onions—you don't have to peel or chop them—makes a great side, punched up with anchovy butter. (The onions are great just tossed with olive oil, too.) You can also make the anchovy butter for other roasted vegetables, or grilled or roasted meats.

SERVES 4

Paprika-anchovy butter
¼ cup [55 g] unsalted butter, at room temperature
5 anchovy fillets, finely chopped
½ small garlic clove, finely chopped
Grated zest and juice of ½ lemon
1 Tbsp finely chopped fresh flat-leaf parsley
¾ tsp paprika
Pinch of chile powder
Fresh black pepper

1½ lb (680 g) small red onions or red pearl onions, unpeeled, halved lengthwise
Pinch of grated piloncillo (see Note, page 58) or dark brown sugar
Pinch of fine sea salt

Heat the oven to 450°F [230°C].

MAKE THE PAPRIKA-ANCHOVY BUTTER: Put the butter, anchovies, garlic, lemon zest and juice, parsley, paprika, chile powder, and a few grinds of black pepper in a medium bowl. Mix with a fork until thoroughly combined.

In a large bowl, rub the onions with the paprika-anchovy butter. Place the onions, cut-side down, on a baking sheet. Roast until the onions are soft and browned, 15 to 25 minutes, depending on their size. Remove from the oven, transfer to a serving dish, sprinkle with piloncillo and sea salt, and serve immediately.

CENTENO SUPER MARKETS

My great-grandmother Jesusita Lopez Centeno started selling groceries out of her small house on Rivas Street, on the West Side of San Antonio, in the mid-1920s. My great-grandfather, Jose "Joe" Centeno Sr., is often credited with founding Centeno Super Markets, the first independent chain of Latino grocery stores in Texas. But it was Jesusita who started it all.

Jesusita Lopez grew up on a farm in Floresville, Texas, and moved to San Antonio when she was twenty-one. She and Joe met while they were both residents of a local boarding house, got married two weeks later, and, over several decades, built a small empire of six supermarkets, two department stores, and a movie theater—their American Dream.

I knew them as Mama and Papa Grande. Papa Grande left Matamoros, Mexico, as a teenager. After a brief stint fighting against the federal army in the Mexican Revolution, he joined the merchant marine and traveled the world instead of following in his father's footsteps to become a doctor. By the time he landed in San Antonio, he could speak English, Italian, Portuguese, and some French, along with his native Spanish. A natural salesman, he could talk to anybody and everybody.

Papa Grande sold suits in downtown San Antonio and was able to buy their little Ribas Street house, where Mama Grande started selling flour, pinto beans, rice, and tomatoes from their front room. This wasn't uncommon at the time, in a neighborhood that had a lot of refugees and not a lot of amenities. Their home became the local ice station, and it grew so busy that they built a small store next door.

For ten years, in the middle of the Great Depression, the two of them ran their little grocery market successfully, largely because Papa Grande built relationships with suppliers for goods that were sometimes hard to come by. In the late '30s, they expanded and built a new superette two blocks away. Families came not only from the neighborhood but also from nearby farms in Pleasanton and Castroville to buy staples for the month: potatoes, pork chops, and lard for making tortillas.

By 1948, Mama and Papa Grande were able to buy an entire city block at Commerce and Las Moras streets, where the first Centeno Super Market opened. It was the largest independent grocery store in Texas at the time. The neighborhood was invited to an open house at 8:30 a.m. on Tuesday, November 9, 1948, a day ahead of the official grand opening.

Customers started lining up early, and by the time the store opened, the entire parking lot was full of people. There were so many that they knocked the doors off the hinges, and you could barely walk through the store. By the end of the day, the entire market had to be restocked for the grand opening.

The day before the open house, Mama Grande was helping some customers who had come in from out-of-town farms and needed their orders, when she slipped and fell. She broke her leg, but she refused to go to the doctor because she didn't want to miss the open house. She was there the whole time, propped up next to a counter to greet customers or at one of the cash registers to ring up groceries. She didn't get a cast until two days later.

Mama Grande was tough as nails and really knew how to hold on to a penny. Driven by a sense of duty to her community, she wanted to provide food for the neighborhood, as well as opportunities to Mexican-Americans who had trouble finding work elsewhere. A newspaper once quoted her on the Latino community in San Antonio: "That's where the money is made, and that's where the money is going back in."

As a Tejano, Mama Grande knew what her shoppers wanted to eat. Centeno Super Market provided Mexican products that saved their customers a trip to the border, 300 mi [483 km] away. Inside the market were a butcher shop and a bakery. Customers cooked every meal at home, usually for big families.

At the butcher shop, one of the most popular cuts of meat was pork shoulder for dishes such as *calabacitas con carne de puerco* (squash and pork stew). Another was round steak, panfried or ground for picadillo. It's hard to believe, but the butchers would make stew meat and hamburger meat out of T-bone steaks or loin strips because people didn't buy them. They wanted to cook meats that were tougher and had more flavor.

A second Centeno Super Market opened in 1968, and then three more in the early '70s. But tragedy struck when my grandfather, Joe Centeno Jr., suddenly died of appendicitis. My great-uncle, much younger than my grandfather, took over the operations. Unprepared for the role, his leadership was shaky at best. Meanwhile, it grew impossible to keep up with the price wars between the growing grocery giants H-E-B and Kroger.

Centeno Super Markets closed for good in 1992 (my great-grandparents had passed away by then). But for seven decades, the markets were an essential part of Tejano cooking in San Antonio.

LA REU

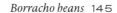

IÓN

These are called *borracho* ("drunken") beans because they're cooked in beer. Borracho beans are a southern Texas–northern Mexico cowboy meal, brothy, with different types of meat—chorizo, ham, bacon, or whatever is around. At family barbecues on Papa Grande's ranch, there would always be a cauldron of beans going, right on the grill, and whoever was barbecuing the meat would just add bits of whatever (kielbasa ends, charred fatty pieces of steak, beef hot dog slices) and pour in beer, which was probably handier than water.

SERVES 8 TO 10

1 lb [455 g] cranberry beans

1 pasilla or ancho chile

½ tsp cumin seeds

8 slices bacon, cut into 1 in [2.5 cm] pieces

1 onion, chopped

1 serrano or jalapeño chile, stemmed, seeded, and finely chopped

2 large garlic cloves, chopped

2 tomatoes, finely diced

1 bunch fresh cilantro (leaves only), finely chopped

4 cups [960 ml] Mexican lager

2½ cups [600 ml] water

1 sprig fresh thyme

1 sprig fresh oregano

1 sprig fresh rosemary

Put the beans in a large stockpot or Dutch oven and add enough water to cover the beans by 2 in [5 cm]. Bring to a rolling boil. Remove from the heat and let the beans sit, covered, for 1 hour.

Meanwhile, using tongs, toast the dried pasilla chile over the open flame of a gas burner until slightly softened and fragrant, about 1 minute. Stem and seed the chile, and cut or tear it into small pieces. Set aside.

Toast the cumin seeds in a small, dry skillet over medium heat, stirring frequently, until fragrant, about 1 minute. Grind to a fine powder with a mortar and pestle or spice grinder and set aside.

When the beans have soaked for 1 hour, drain, rinse, and set aside. Cook the bacon in the same pot over medium-high heat, stirring frequently, just until the fat is rendered and the bacon is browned at the edges but still quite soft, 4 to 5 minutes.

Add the onion, serrano, and garlic, and cook, stirring occasionally, until the onion is translucent, 2 to 3 minutes. Add the tomatoes, cilantro,

CONT'D

the toasted cumin, and the toasted chile and stir to combine. Add the drained beans, beer, and 2½ cups [600 ml] water.

Tie the thyme, oregano, and rosemary sprigs into a bundle with kitchen string and drop it into the pot. Bring to a boil, lower the heat to low, and simmer, stirring occasionally, until the beans are very tender (depending on the age of the beans, this could take 1½ to 2½ hours) and the broth has thickened. If the liquid seems low before the beans are cooked through, add a little water, ¼ cup [60 ml] at a time. Discard the tied herbs and serve immediately. Leftover beans will keep in a covered container in the refrigerator for up to 5 days. Reheat before serving.

Borracho beans make good refried beans. They're great as a side, with huevos rancheros, or in breakfast tacos with cheese and bacon, a personal favorite. They're great with everything, really. The additional bacon gives the beans extra oomph. I have a *machacador* for smashing the beans as they cook, but a potato masher or the back of a spoon work, too.

SERVES 4 TO 6

2 slices bacon, cut crosswise into ⅛ in [4 mm] strips

2 Tbsp finely chopped onion

2 ½ cups [about 600 g] borracho beans (page 145),
including a little bit of the liquid

Finely grated cheddar cheese for garnish

Heat a large cast-iron skillet over medium heat and add the bacon. Cook to render the fat and get the edges just a little crispy and slightly browned, 2 minutes. Add the onion and cook until translucent, 2 to 3 minutes.

Add the beans along with a little bit of their liquid. (The liquid will reduce and help to achieve a slightly creamy consistency.) Using the back of a spoon or a *machacador*, smash all of the beans, stirring occasionally and adjusting the heat as necessary so they don't scorch. Cook until the liquid is reduced and the beans are creamy, 10 to 12 minutes. If you want the beans even creamier, transfer them to a blender while still hot and pulse.

Serve immediately with grated cheese on top.

My mom's rice was requested at all family gatherings. The key to making Mexican red rice is to toast the grains briefly first, so they won't stick together and will puff up during cooking. That first sauté also gives the rice a slightly nutty flavor. My mom's secret ingredient is V8 vegetable juice, which gives it loads of flavor.

SERVES 6 TO 8 (MAKES 5½ CUPS / 850 G)

2 Tbsp avocado oil

2 cups [400 g] good-quality long-grain rice (we use Anson Mills Carolina Gold)

1 large shallot, or ¼ large onion, finely chopped

2 garlic cloves, minced

1 ½ cups [360 ml] V8 vegetable juice

3 cups [720 ml] vegetable broth, chicken broth, or water

¼ tsp fine sea salt

2 Tbsp finely chopped fresh flat-leaf parsley leaves

2 Tbsp finely chopped fresh cilantro leaves

Heat the oil in a sauté or other high-sided pan, preferably nonstick, over medium-high heat until hot and shimmering. Add the rice and toast, stirring occasionally, until light gold, about 5 minutes. Add the shallot and garlic, and sauté until fragrant, 1 minute.

Add the V8, vegetable broth, and salt. Bring to a boil, lower the heat to low, cover, and simmer until the liquid is fully absorbed. Keep an eye on it; if it's absorbed before the rice is tender, add a little more stock, starting with a few tablespoons. Fluff the rice with a fork and stir in the parsley and cilantro. Serve immediately.

I grew up with a lot of barbecued chicken. I wanted to make a roast chicken with similar flavors—smoky, spicy, and tangy. First the chicken is rubbed with a chile paste made with guajillo chiles, hoja santa leaves, and onion. Toward the end of roasting, it's glazed with hot sauce and butter.

SERVES 4

One 3 to 3 ½ lb [1.4 to 1.6 kg] whole chicken

1 tsp fine sea salt

½ tsp fresh black pepper

½ cup [110 g] cold unsalted butter, cut into thin slices

5 sprigs fresh thyme

1 lemon, quartered

¼ cup [60 ml] cobjini (page 41)

2 Tbsp unsalted butter

½ cup [120 ml] vinegar-based arbol or chipotle hot sauce, such as Cholula

Cabbage and kale slaw

¼ head green cabbage, cored and sliced ⅛ in [4 mm] thick

2 large kale leaves, stemmed, rolled, and cut into thin ribbons

2 Tbsp finely chopped fresh mint, cilantro, or parsley leaves, or a combination

¼ cup [60 ml] oregano vinaigrette (page 21)

Heat the oven to 400°F [200°C].

Season the chicken with the salt and pepper all over as well as inside the cavity. Slide the butter slices between the skin and the breast and thigh meat. Stuff the cavity with the thyme sprigs and quartered lemon. Rub the cobjini over the chicken, inside and out.

Tuck the wings behind the back of the chicken. Take a piece of kitchen string about four times the length of the bird and wrap it twice around the legs at the ankles, so that you're left with two long ends. Take both ends of the string and pull the string over the breast (toward the neck). Turn the bird over and crisscross the string across its back. Turn the bird over again and bring the string back to the legs, tying it off at the ankles.

Put the chicken, breast-side up, in a roasting pan and roast until the skin is crisp and lightly browned, 15 to 20 minutes. Lower the heat to 325°F [165°C]. Continue to roast until the internal temperature of the chicken reaches 150°F [66° C] on a meat or instant-read thermometer inserted into the thickest part of the thigh, about 45 minutes.

Meanwhile, melt the butter with the hot sauce in a small saucepan over medium heat. Brush the baste all over the chicken every 5 minutes until the chicken reaches 165°F [74°C]. Remove from the oven and let rest for 15 minutes.

MAKE THE CABBAGE AND KALE SLAW: Toss the cabbage, kale, and herbs with the oregano vinaigrette in a large bowl. Transfer the chicken to a platter. Serve immediately with the cabbage and kale slaw.

For juicy, crunchy fried chicken with great flavor, I first make a special brine with buttermilk and a little Japanese *shio koji* (fermented rice seasoning) which is itself a great umami-packed marinade. I also use a lot of spices for the coating. The texture of this dredge was inspired by the fried chicken I grew up with, Church's Chicken, a fast-food chain that began in San Antonio. It had a sort of fluffy-crunchy exterior, so I added baking soda and baking powder to the dredge for a light crunch.

NOTE: Shio koji is available at Japanese markets and online.

SERVES 6

One 3½ lb [1.6 kg] whole chicken

Buttermilk marinade
1 cup [240 ml] buttermilk
⅓ cup [80 ml] shio koji, or 1½ tsp fine sea salt
1 garlic clove, grated with a rasp-style grater
2 egg whites
2 Tbsp vodka
2 Tbsp olive oil
2 Tbsp miso
1 Tbsp sesame oil

Coating
3 cups [405 g] all-purpose flour
1 cup [140 g] cornstarch
1½ Tbsp baking powder
1 tsp baking soda
1 Tbsp garlic powder
1 Tbsp dry mustard
1 Tbsp ground ginger
1 Tbsp fine sea salt
1½ tsp smoked paprika
1½ tsp celery salt
1½ tsp dried thyme
1½ tsp dried Mexican oregano, preferably Oregano Indio (see Note, page 17)
½ tsp freshly ground black pepper

Vegetable oil (such as avocado or grapeseed) or peanut oil for frying
7 or 8 fresh mint leaves for garnish
¼ cup [85 g] honey for garnish

153

CONT'D

CUT THE CHICKEN INTO PIECES: Remove the legs from the chicken, and cut through the joint between each drumstick and thigh to separate them. Cut the wings from the breast. Cut the breast in half, and cut each half into three equal pieces, all bones intact. You should have twelve pieces. Set aside.

MAKE THE MARINADE: Combine the buttermilk, koji, garlic, egg whites, vodka, olive oil, miso, and sesame oil in a large bowl and whisk to blend. Put the chicken pieces in the marinade. Marinate in the refrigerator for at least 2 hours and up to 6 hours. Remove the chicken from the refrigerator 30 minutes before frying and let sit at room temperature.

MAKE THE COATING: With a whisk or fork, mix the flour, cornstarch, baking powder, baking soda, garlic powder, mustard, ginger, salt, smoked paprika, celery salt, thyme, oregano, and black pepper in a large bowl.

With one hand, remove a piece of chicken from the buttermilk. With the other hand (so that you always keep one hand fairly clean and dry), toss the chicken in the flour mixture so it's lightly coated. Set aside on a baking sheet, and repeat with the remaining pieces of chicken.

Dredge each of the chicken pieces in the flour mixture again and set aside.

Pour enough oil into a Dutch oven or other heavy-bottom pot so that it comes almost halfway up the sides. Heat the oil over medium-high heat to 365°F [185°C] on a candy or deep-fry thermometer. The heat will drop when you put the chicken in—you want it to be about 350°F [180°C] while you're frying. Fry in batches until the chicken's internal temp reaches 175°F [79°C] on an instant-read thermometer and the breading is golden brown (don't let it get too dark), 8 to 10 minutes, turning the chicken over about halfway through cooking. Transfer to a rack on a baking sheet. Make sure the oil is hot enough before adding the next batch of chicken.

Transfer the chicken to a platter, tear the mint leaves over the chicken, and drizzle with honey. Serve immediately.

It was at Threadgills in Austin that I first had a revelatory chicken-fried steak. My tía Alice Jo lived in Austin for a while. During a visit, when I was twelve years old, I helped Uncle Keith work on the Mustang he was over-hauling. As thanks for pulling the carpet out of the car and scraping all the glue off the floor, they took me to Threadgills for chicken-fried steak, and I never forgot it. The steak was tender, and the coating, extra crunchy. It was as big as a platter.

SERVES 4 TO 6

Bacon gravy
1 Tbsp unsalted butter
1 Tbsp all-purpose flour
3 slices bacon, cut into ½ in [12 mm] pieces
¼ cup [30 g] finely chopped onion
3 garlic cloves, finely chopped
2 cups [480 ml] milk
1 tsp fine sea salt
Fresh black pepper
2 tsp Amá spice mix (page 32) or chile powder (optional)

¾ cup [180 ml] buttermilk
Fine sea salt and fresh black pepper
Four 8 to 9 oz [230 to 255 g] cube steaks
1½ cups [205 g] all-purpose flour
½ cup [70 g] cornstarch
Pinch chile powder
¼ tsp baking powder
¼ tsp baking soda
1½ cups [360 ml] whole milk
2 eggs
½ cup [120 ml] vegetable oil (such as avocado or grapeseed),
or peanut oil for frying
1 Tbsp red-eye spice (page 36, optional)

Heat the oven to 325°F [165°C].

MAKE THE BACON GRAVY: In a small bowl, knead the butter and flour together and set aside. Cook the bacon in a medium heavy-bottom skillet over medium-high heat until the fat renders, the edges are just browned, and the bacon is still soft, 3 to 5 minutes. Add the onion and garlic and cook until the onion is translucent, 2 to 3 minutes. Whisk in the milk, salt, a few grinds of black pepper, and the spice mix, if using. Whisk in the butter-flour mixture and cook, stirring frequently, until the gravy is nappe (coats the back of a spoon) and there is no raw-flour taste, 5 minutes. Keep the gravy warm over low heat.

CONT'D

Mix the buttermilk with ¼ tsp salt and a few grinds of black pepper in a large bowl. Add the steaks to the bowl, turn to coat, and set aside.

Whisk together the flour, cornstarch, chile powder, 1 tsp salt, a few grinds of black pepper, the baking powder, and baking soda in a large bowl and set aside.

Whisk together the milk and eggs in a third large bowl until blended.

Heat the oil in a high-sided, heavy-bottom sauté pan or Dutch oven over high heat until the temperature reaches 375°F [190°C] on a deep-fry or instant-read thermometer. (You can also insert the handle of a wooden spoon into the oil so that it touches the bottom of the pan. When small bubbles come up the sides of the spoon, the oil is hot enough.)

While the oil is heating, dredge one of the steaks: Remove a steak from the buttermilk, shaking off any excess. Using one hand, dredge the steak in the flour to lightly coat it, shaking off the excess. With the other hand (so that one hand stays fairly clean and dry), gently dip it into the egg mixture, shaking off the excess, then pass the steak through the bowl of flour again so that it is evenly coated (if the coating clumps, it's OK).

When the oil is hot, fry the first side of the steak until crispy and golden brown—you'll see crispy brown edges on the sides of the steak, 3 to 5 minutes. Using tongs, flip the steak gently away from you, so that oil doesn't splatter on you. Fry the second side until crispy and golden brown, another 3 to 5 minutes. Place a rack on a baking sheet or line it with paper towels. Transfer the steak to the baking sheet to drain. Repeat with the remaining steaks.

Remove any paper towels, and place the baking sheet in the oven to warm the steaks, 4 to 6 minutes. Transfer to a platter, pour over the bacon gravy, and sprinkle with the red-eye spice, if using. Serve immediately.

This recipe is for Uncle Keith, who loves his steak black and blue, very charred on the outside, rare on the inside, and cool to the touch (the internal temperature should be 100°F to 110°F [38°C to 43°C]). The onions for the onion rings are sliced paper-thin, like at Jim's, where my family in San Antonio sometimes goes for burgers.

NOTE : The pan or grill needs to be smoking hot over high heat, and kept hot during the entire cooking process. Keep the exhaust fan on high and windows open if cooking inside as it will cause a lot of smoke.

SERVES 4

Buttermilk onion rings

2 cups [480 ml] buttermilk

1 large white onion, sliced crosswise into paper-thin rings on a mandoline

3 cups [405 g] all-purpose flour

Fine sea salt

1 Tbsp fresh black pepper

Vegetable oil (such as avocado or grapeseed) or peanut oil for frying

1 Tbsp paprika

1 Tbsp ground coffee

1 Tbsp Amá spice mix (page 32) or chile powder

2 tsp fine sea salt

1 tsp onion powder

1 tsp garlic powder

1 tsp white pepper

1 tsp black pepper

½ tsp dried thyme

½ tsp dried Mexican oregano, preferably Oregano Indio (see Note, page 17)

4 Tbsp avocado or peanut oil

Two 1 lb [455 g] New York steaks, about 1 in [2.5 cm] thick

2 Tbsp unsalted butter

4 garlic cloves, crushed

2 sprigs fresh rosemary

½ cup [60 g] crumbled blue cheese

MAKE THE ONION RINGS: Pour the buttermilk into a medium bowl, add the onion, and steep in the buttermilk for 2 to 3 hours in the refrigerator. In another medium bowl, whisk together the flour, 1 Tbsp salt, and pepper, and set aside.

Fill a large pot with enough oil to come nearly halfway up the sides. Heat the oil over medium-high heat until the temperature on a candy or deep-fry thermometer reaches 350°F [180°C].

Remove the onions from the buttermilk, shaking off the excess. Toss the rings gently in the seasoned flour for a nice even coating, shaking off any excess flour. Fry the onion rings, a few handfuls at a time, in the hot oil until golden brown, 2 to 3 minutes.

Remove the onions from the oil with a spider or slotted spoon to a paper towel–lined bowl and toss with a pinch of salt. Keep them in the oven, heated to the lowest setting, if you like.

Heat a large cast-iron skillet with a lid over high heat for at least 5 minutes, either on a burner or an outdoor grill. You need extremely high heat, 500°F [260°C] or higher, to cook a steak black and blue.

Mix the paprika, coffee, spice mix, salt, onion powder, garlic powder, white pepper, black pepper, thyme, and oregano in a small bowl. Rub 1 Tbsp of the oil on each steak and season generously with the spice mixture on both sides.

When the pan is smoking hot, add 1 Tbsp oil and immediately and gently, place a steak in the skillet away from you so the oil doesn't spatter on you. Keep the steak in the pan over high heat for 1½ minutes, or just until it takes on a good char. Flip the steak using tongs and cook for another 1½ minutes, so both sides have a significantly charred crust.

Add 1 Tbsp of the butter, 2 of the garlic cloves, and 1 sprig of rosemary to the pan. Baste the steak with the butter for 1 minute. Cover the pan with a lid or cover the grill and cook for 1 minute more. Remove from the heat and transfer the contents of the pan to a platter to rest. Repeat to cook the second steak.

Sprinkle the onion rings with the blue cheese. After the steaks have rested for a few minutes, slice and serve immediately with the onion rings.

For a while, when I was a kid, my dad worked at Centeno Super Market managing the store's meat department, and he was fond of the fajita cut of skirt steak. The word *fajita* is the diminutive of *faja*, which is the Spanish word for "belt," a reference to the diaphragm muscle on a steer, where a skirt steak comes from. It was the cut, along with the head, used by rancheros in south Texas, who would grill it, cut it up, and eat it on flour tortillas. Later it was simple backyard grilling food—Tex-Mex right over the fire, hot and fast. Fajitas at our house meant Dad was going all out. Whenever I saw a metal roasting tray on the kitchen counter piled with skirt steak, along with green onions and a bottle of Worcestershire sauce (the key ingredient, along with limes, for his marinade), I knew it was on. There would be pico de gallo and guacamole, and flour tortillas. There would be Big Red. Potato chips and Fritos (also a San Antonio thing). And probably kielbasa and grilled chicken, too.

SERVES 4

¼ onion, grated on the largest holes of a box grater

5 garlic cloves, sliced

¼ cup plus 2 Tbsp [90 ml] olive oil

1 tsp fine sea salt

Juice of 2 limes

3 Tbsp Worcestershire sauce

Fresh black pepper

2 lb [910 g] skirt steak

8 green onions

8 to 12 flour tortillas for serving, homemade (page 59) or store-bought, warmed in a skillet over medium heat

Stir together the onion, garlic, ¼ cup [60 ml] of the olive oil, the salt, lime juice, Worcestershire sauce, and several grinds of black pepper in a large bowl. Add the steak, cover, and marinate in the refrigerator for at least 1 hour and up to 6 hours.

Heat a grill to high heat. Remove the steak from the refrigerator and set aside.

Rub the green onions with the remaining 2 Tbsp olive oil. Grill over high heat until charred, 2 to 3 minutes. Move to a cooler part of the grill and put them on a piece of foil to keep warm while the steaks cook.

Grill the steaks over high heat until seared on one side, with grill marks, about 1½ minutes. Turn 90 degrees to get crosshatched marks, another 1½ minutes. (This helps to cook the steaks evenly.) Flip and repeat on the second side. If the steaks aren't cooked through, move them to a cooler part of the grill to finish cooking, or place on top of foil to cook more slowly, an additional 2 to 4 minutes.

Remove the green onions and steaks from the grill. Let the steaks rest for about 5 minutes, and then cut them against the grain into ¾ in [2 cm] thick slices. Transfer the onions and steaks to a platter and serve with warm flour tortillas.

Fajitas are traditionally made with skirt steak, but once people started using other cuts, all bets were off. In the 1970s, restaurants all over Texas marketed sizzling fajitas of all kinds. (The dirty secret of a lot of those sizzling fajita platters was someone standing at the pass with a squeeze bottle, waiting to squirt a little water onto each iron platter so it would go out to the table steaming and hissing.) Shrimp and chicken options became common. I'm OK with that; I like the fajita treatment for any kind of meat or seafood, really, which means serving it with hot sauce, limes, avocados or guacamole, and warm flour tortillas. These are a riff on chicken fajitas, which are often marinated in lime juice and spices. Here, the marinade is made with freshly grated ginger and turmeric, which aren't the usual Tex-Mex flavors. But they're great with chicken, which comes out a vibrant golden color from the turmeric.

SERVES 4 TO 6

2 lb [910 g] boneless, skinless chicken breasts

1 serrano chile, stemmed

1 knob [25 g] fresh turmeric, peeled and grated

1 knob [35 g] fresh ginger, grated

2 fresh bay leaves (optional; don't substitute dry)

2 garlic cloves, chopped

Fine sea salt and fresh black pepper

¼ cup plus 2 Tbsp [90 ml] olive oil

Juice of 1 lime

1 onion, cut into ½ in [12 mm] rings

3 poblano chiles, halved lengthwise, stemmed, and seeded

8 to 12 flour tortillas, homemade (page 59) or store-bought, warmed in a skillet over medium heat

Mexican salmorejo (page 28) for serving

BUTTERFLY THE CHICKEN BREASTS: Put a chicken breast on your cutting board. With one hand flat on top of it, carefully cut into the side of the breast horizontally with a sharp knife, *almost* all the way through, but leaving a hinge so it will open like a book. Repeat with each breast.

Open the breasts and lightly score the breasts all over with the tip of a sharp knife to help the marinade penetrate the meat.

Chop the serrano chile. For less heat, first remove the seeds and ribs, rinse the chile under cold water, and pat dry.

Put the turmeric, ginger, bay leaves (if using), serrano, garlic, 1 tsp salt, a few grinds of pepper, ¼ cup [60 ml] of the olive oil, and the lime juice in a food processor and pulse until blended but still nice and chunky. (Be sure the garlic is fully processed.) Transfer to a medium bowl. Alternatively, you can make the marinade by dicing the bay leaves, serrano, and garlic and then mixing the ingredients together in a bowl with a fork.

CONT'D

Put the chicken in the marinade, and turn to coat. Cover and marinate in the refrigerator for at least 1 hour and up to 6 hours.

Heat a grill to medium-high heat. Remove the chicken from the refrigerator and set aside.

Rub the onion rings with 1 Tbsp of the olive oil, keeping the rounds intact. Sprinkle with a pinch of salt and a couple of grinds of pepper. Rub the poblano chiles with the remaining 1 Tbsp olive oil. Sprinkle with a pinch of salt and a couple of grinds of black pepper.

Grill the onion rounds and poblanos until charred and cooked through, 2 to 3 minutes per side. Move to a cooler part of the grill and place on a piece of foil to keep warm while the chicken cooks.

Grill one side of the chicken until seared, with grill marks, and the chicken releases easily, 2 to 3 minutes. Turn 90 degrees so there are cross-hatched marks and the chicken cooks evenly, another 2 to 3 minutes. Flip and repeat on the second side. Make sure the chicken is cooked through (a meat or instant-read thermometer should reach 165°F [74°C]). If it's not done, move it to a cooler part of the grill to finish cooking, or place on top of foil to cook more slowly, an additional 2 to 4 minutes. Cut the chicken and poblanos into 1 in [2.5 cm] slices, transfer to a platter, and serve with the onions, warm flour tortillas, and Mexican salmorejo.

Shrimp are great for grilling, so why not serve them like fajitas? These are punched up with hot sriracha, lime, and fish sauce.

SERVES 4 TO 6

Marinade

½ medium white onion

5 garlic cloves

3 Tbsp Mexican sriracha (page 29) or
adobo sauce from canned chipotles in adobo

Zest and juice of 1 lime, plus 2 limes, quartered

2 Tbsp fish sauce

2 Tbsp olive oil

½ tsp fine sea salt

2 lb [910 g] shrimp (16/20 count), shelled and deveined

Fresh black pepper

8 green onions (white and green parts)

2 Tbsp olive oil

8 to 12 flour tortillas, homemade (page 59) or store-bought,
warmed in a skillet over medium heat

1 bunch fresh cilantro (leaves only), finely chopped

MAKE THE MARINADE: Grate the onion on the smallest holes of a box grater into a large bowl (you should have about ¼ cup [65 g]). Grate the garlic with a rasp-style grater into the same bowl. Add the sriracha, lime zest and juice, fish sauce, olive oil, and salt. Stir to combine.

Pour the marinade into a large plastic zip bag or bowl or container and add the shrimp. Marinate in the refrigerator for at least 1 hour and up to 3 hours.

    Heat a grill to medium heat. Remove the shrimp from the refrigerator and add a few grinds of pepper; set aside.

    Rub the green onions with the 2 Tbsp of olive oil. Grill on high heat until charred, 2 to 3 minutes. Move the green onions to a cooler part of the grill or put them on a piece of foil to keep warm while the shrimp cooks.

    Put the shrimp on the grill and cook until they turn opaque and begin to curl, 2 or 3 minutes per side. Transfer the shrimp to a platter. Serve with the warm flour tortillas, along with the charred green onions, cilantro, and quartered limes wedges for garnish.

I've always loved pork with anchovies. Here the anchovies add a lot of umami to the marinade for the grilled pork, and they stand up to the other assertive flavors—the chiles, garlic, and lime.

SERVES 4 TO 6

4 pasilla de Oaxaca or dried New Mexico chiles,
or 2 to 4 ancho chiles, stemmed and seeded

2 anchovy fillets, chopped

2 garlic cloves, finely chopped

4 Tbsp olive oil

Juice of 1 lime

Fine sea salt

2 lb [910 g] boneless pork butt, cut into ½ in [12 mm] thick slices,
or 2 lb [910 g] boneless pork chops, ½ in [12 mm] thick

1 onion, cut into ½ in [12 mm] rings

Fresh black pepper

3 poblano chiles, halved lengthwise, stemmed, and seeded

8 to 12 flour tortillas, homemade (page 59) or store-bought,
warmed in a skillet over medium heat

Put the pasilla de Oaxaca chiles in a small saucepan and add just enough water to cover. Bring to a boil. Remove from the heat and drain the chiles, discarding the liquid.

Put the chiles on a cutting board and chop finely. Transfer to a large bowl. Add the anchovies, garlic, 2 Tbsp olive oil, lime juice, and ¼ tsp salt. Put the pork in the marinade and turn to coat the meat thoroughly. Cover with plastic wrap and marinate in the refrigerator for at least 1 hour and up to 6 hours.

Heat a grill to medium-high heat. Remove the pork from the refrigerator and set aside.

Rub the rounds of onions, keeping them intact, with 1 Tbsp olive oil. Sprinkle with a pinch of salt and a couple of grinds of black pepper. Rub the poblano chiles with the remaining 1 Tbsp olive oil. Sprinkle with a pinch of salt and a couple of grinds of black pepper.

Grill the onion rounds and poblanos until charred and cooked through, 2 to 3 minutes per side, then move them away from the hottest part of the grill onto a piece of foil to keep warm while the pork cooks.

Grill one side of the pork over medium-high heat just until seared, with grill marks, about 2 minutes. Turn 90 degrees so that there are cross-hatched marks, another 2 minutes. Flip and repeat on the opposite side. A meat or instant-read thermometer should reach 145°F [63°C]. If the pork isn't cooked through, move it to a cooler part of the grill to finish cooking, or place the pork on a piece of foil to cook more slowly, an additional 2 to 4 minutes. Cut the pork into 1 in [2.5 cm] strips, transfer to a platter, and serve with onions, poblanos, and warm flour tortillas.

THE RANCH

In the late 1930s, Jose "Joe" Centeno Sr.—Papa Grande—bought a 200-acre [81-hectare] farm halfway between San Antonio and a small town to the south called Poteet. Mama Grande was a Spanish-Polish farm girl from Floresville, Texas, and she was really in her element there. (She didn't drive a car, but she did drive a tractor.) She grew watermelons, cantaloupes, and Mexican squash called *tatuma*, and tended to chickens, cows, hogs, horses, donkeys, ducks, and several fat Weimaraners. In addition to her farming skills, she made the best potato salad and the hottest hot sauce, which she ate by the spoonful as if it was soup.

Four generations of Centenos spent weekends at the farm for Sunday barbecues, family softball games, and holiday blowouts. Everyone called it "the ranch." On a normal weekend, there might be thirty to fifty people there, and for special occasions, the number ran into the hundreds. The entire family and all of the employees of the Centeno Super Markets used to come on Easter to play flag football and eat ribs, T-bones, ranch-style beans, and big bowlfuls of Mama Grande's potato salad.

My dad practically grew up on the ranch, where he liked running around in his Davy Crockett hat and feeding the chickens. We still went out there when I was a kid, mostly for special occasions. Manuel, a butcher from the Commerce Street store who gave my dad his first lessons in cutting meat, manned the barbecue pit. He was the toughest, meanest, shortest guy, who drank a lot and fought a lot and was like one of the family. Later it was a vaquero named Juan, also tough as heck. (One time the city had some trees cut down in front of one of the supermarkets. He and my great uncle were so upset about it that they went down to city hall with a chainsaw and attempted to cut down one of its trees. They had only cut a few branches before they were arrested.)

Papa Grande's pit was a cement round set over a 4 ft [1.2 m] hole in the ground. The cement had been molded to look like a tree trunk, which had a "branch" with a pulley that lowered and raised the grill. There was something like a chimney grate where men would shovel in mesquite and oak wood already on fire. That would be for steaks and ribs and chickens. A 10 ft [3 m] long flat grill was dedicated to burgers and *tripas*.

The pit was big enough for cabrito, milk-fed goat wrapped and cooked in banana leaves; and barbacoa, steer heads prepared the same way. The cabrito came from Mr. Doria, a family friend who started raising goats in Stockdale, just outside of San Antonio, after cabrito became popular beyond the border town of Laredo. The steer were from the first organic herd of cattle in San Antonio—roaming, grass-fed steer that were never put on feed. They were slaughtered in our own slaughterhouse in Seguin.

These were meals that I took for granted as a kid, sitting at the big outdoor picnic table under a thatched roof near the barbecue pit. Beyond the live oaks and the peach trees, I could see the outlines of buildings in downtown San Antonio. Those glory days of the ranch didn't last forever. Once the stores went under, the ranch was sold off. But it was a big part of the life of our family for a long time. It inspired many of the items on the menu at Bar Amá, including what we call La Reunión specials. The ranch lives on in good times.

My tía Alice Jo makes this shoulder roast almost every weekend. She loves it, and I do, too. It's slow-cooked until the meat is tender, with some crunchy caramelized fatty bits. I think of it as a cross between porchetta and carnitas. I really like the mix of chipotle, curry, garlic, and rosemary—unique flavors that taste great in a tortilla.

SERVES 6 TO 8

1 large sprig fresh rosemary

6 garlic cloves

1 Tbsp Madras curry powder

1 tsp chipotle chile powder

1 tsp fine sea salt

¼ cup [60 ml] olive oil

One 3 lb [1.4 kg] pork shoulder, with fat cap, preferably bone-in

Flour tortillas for serving, homemade (page 59) or store-bought, or corn tortillas, warmed in a skillet over medium heat

2 avocados, pitted, peeled, and cut into a large dice

Your favorite hot sauce for serving

Remove the leaves from the rosemary sprig and put them in a blender. Add the garlic, curry powder, chipotle powder, salt, and olive oil. Blend until smooth and set aside.

Place the pork on a clean work surface, fat-side up. With the tip of a small sharp knife, score the fat, without cutting into the meat.

Rub the spice blend into the scored fat and all over the pork roast. Put it in the refrigerator to marinate for at least 4 hours and up to 12 hours.

Heat the oven to 425°F [220°C]. Remove the pork from the refrigerator about 1 hour before you want to cook it, and let it come to room temperature.

Put a rack in a roasting pan, and place the pork, fat-side up, on the rack. Add enough water to come up the sides of the pan by about ½ in [12 mm]. (This prevents dripping fat from burning on the bottom of the pan; add water as needed.) Roast for 30 minutes, so the top starts crisping up.

Lower the heat to 325°F [165°C]. Remove the pork from the oven, cover with a double layer of foil, and pop it back in the oven to roast for another 4½ hours, or until the pork is very soft and tender. Transfer to a platter and shred into chunks. Serve with the warm tortillas, diced avocado, and hot sauce.

These are easy party ribs, inspired by Nana's crispy charred ribs, which she broiled in the oven. Instead of a rack, she'd cook thin chops with rib bones attached, or occasionally, random single rib bones from the butcher (no chops, or barely any meat at all!). She'd brush them with ketchup and a little chile powder and throw them in the oven. That was it. I use Bar Amá's dry rub, which has a molasses-like flavor from the brown sugar, and BBQ sauce with a chipotle kick. And then slow-roast.

SERVES 4 TO 8

1 or 2 racks of baby back ribs

Dry rub
1 ¾ cups [350 g] packed dark brown sugar
2 tsp fine sea salt
2 tsp Amá spice mix (page 32) or chipotle chile powder
2 tsp smoked paprika
2 tsp fresh black pepper
2 tsp ground cumin
2 tsp dried Mexican oregano, preferably Oregano Indio (see Note, page 17)
1 tsp dry mustard
1 tsp ground coriander
1 tsp chile flakes
½ tsp ground cinnamon

Bar Amá BBQ sauce
¾ cup [195 g] ketchup
⅓ cup [80 ml] water
¼ cup [60 ml] apple cider vinegar
½ small yellow onion, finely chopped
2 garlic cloves, grated with a rasp-style grater
1 Tbsp adobo sauce from canned chipotles in adobo
1 Tbsp Amá spice mix (page 32) or chile powder
2 tsp olive oil
1 tsp chile powder
1 tsp dried Mexican oregano, preferably Oregano Indio (see Note, page 17)
1 tsp Worcestershire sauce
½ tsp ground cumin
½ tsp dry mustard
¼ tsp fine sea salt

CONT'D

Put the rib racks on a foil-lined baking sheet and set aside.

MAKE THE DRY RUB: Mix together the brown sugar, salt, spice mix, smoked paprika, black pepper, cumin, oregano, mustard, coriander, chile flakes, and cinnamon in a medium bowl. Set aside 1 Tbsp for the barbecue sauce, and rub the rest all over the ribs. Refrigerate for 1 hour.

Heat the oven to 300°F [150°C].
Wrap the ribs well in foil and cook until tender (the tip of a knife should slide easily into the meat), 2 to 3 hours.

MAKE THE BBQ SAUCE: In a medium bowl, mix the ketchup, water, apple cider vinegar, onion, garlic, dry rub, adobo, spice mix, olive oil, chile powder, oregano, Worcestershire sauce, cumin, mustard, and salt until thoroughly combined. Stir in the reserved 1 Tbsp of rub.
About 30 minutes before the ribs finish cooking, remove the foil and brush them with the barbecue sauce. Brush them two more times with the barbecue sauce before removing them from the oven.

Slice the ribs between the bones, transfer to a platter, and serve immediately.

A
M
Á

On Thanksgiving and Christmas we often ate smoked turkey special-ordered from Ms. Miller's BBQ or from Mr. Kelly's 24-hour BBQ King. Or Grandma Alice cooked the turkey, which she brined with beer and rubbed with chile butter—giving it so much flavor that nobody missed the smoke. Grandma Alice was widowed young and spent most of her adult life working, but when she was in her late sixties and retired, she was cooking for us grandkids. She loved Thanksgiving and would cook two or three young hens instead of one giant Tom. Her turkey was always juicy because her brine kept it moist. For a Tex-Mex turkey, the brine should have plenty of flavor—I like chiles, brown sugar, herbs, and lots of garlic. The chile butter does double duty as a baste and a component of the gravy.

SERVES 8

Six 12 oz [360 ml] cans or bottles of Mexican beer,
such as Pacifico

8 cups [2 L] water

1 cup plus 2 ½ tsp [315 g] fine sea salt

½ cup [100 g] packed dark brown sugar

6 ancho chiles

4 heads garlic, halved

1 orange, unpeeled, cut into slices

1 Tbsp dried Mexican oregano, preferably Oregano Indio (see Note, page 17)

4 or 5 sprigs fresh thyme

2 sprigs fresh rosemary

One 12 lb [5.5 kg] turkey

Chile butter

2 ancho chiles

2 pasilla chiles

2 dried arbol chiles

2 cups [480 ml] water

1 cup [220 g] unsalted butter

Gravy

1 cup [240 ml] dry white wine

¼ cup [35 g] all-purpose flour

2 cups [480 ml] chicken stock or broth

Salt and fresh black pepper

CONT'D

173

To make the turkey brine, combine the beer, water, salt, brown sugar, chiles, garlic, orange slices, oregano, thyme, and rosemary in a large pot or Dutch oven. Bring to a simmer over medium-high heat and simmer until the salt and sugar are completely dissolved. Remove from the heat, cover with a lid, and cool at room temperature for 30 minutes. Refrigerate until completely cool, about 2 hours.

Put the turkey in a large container or brining bag and pour the brine over the turkey. Refrigerate for 24 hours. Flip the turkey once, about halfway through brining.

Remove the turkey from the brine and pat dry with paper towels. Strain the brine, discarding the liquid. Put the remaining solids—the chiles, orange slices, herbs, and garlic—into the cavity of the turkey. Transfer to a rack and air-dry the turkey for 2 hours at room temperature. (You can dry it for longer in the refrigerator—up to 24 hours—but make sure to take it out 2 hours before roasting.)

Heat the oven to 375°F [190°C].

To roast the turkey, put a rack in a heavy-bottom roasting pan, and put the turkey on the rack. Add enough water to the pan so that it comes ¼ in [6 mm] up the sides. (This will help keep the drippings from burning; add more water as needed.)

Roast for 30 minutes, and then reduce the oven temperature to 325°F [165°C]. Roast until a meat or instant-read thermometer inserted into the thickest part of the thigh meat reaches 165°F [74°C], about 1 hour and 20 minutes more.

MAKE THE CHILE BUTTER: Stem and seed the ancho, pasilla, and arbol chiles. Put them in a small saucepan, add the water, and bring to a boil. Remove from the heat and let sit for 10 minutes so that the chiles completely soften. Drain, remove the chiles from the pan, and set aside. In the same saucepan, melt the butter. Remove from the heat and cool until just warm. Put the butter and chiles in a blender or food processor and blend to combine. Put the mixture in a saucepan and keep warm on the stove.

Start basting the turkey once its internal temperature reaches 145°F [63°C], sometime during the last 30 minutes of roasting. Set aside ¼ cup [60 ml] of the butter for the gravy, and brush the remaining chile butter all over the turkey every 5 minutes or so.

Transfer the turkey to a platter and let rest for 30 minutes.

MAKE THE GRAVY: Put the roasting pan across two burners on medium-high heat. Add the reserved chile butter and the wine, stir into the pan drippings, and cook, scraping up the browned bits with a wooden spoon, until the liquid thickens, about 10 minutes. Add the flour and cook, stirring, for 1 to 2 minutes.

Gradually add the stock and simmer, stirring frequently, until the gravy thickens more and doesn't taste floury, 5 to 8 minutes. If desired, strain through a fine-mesh sieve. Pour into a gravy dish and season with salt and pepper. Serve immediately with the roast turkey.

Chili may be the state dish of Texas, a legacy of the chili queens of San Antonio, who famously set up their stands on the city's plazas beginning in the 1880s, but I admit that I rarely make it—except the day after Thanksgiving, when I honor my friend Octavio Rodriguez, whom the world lost too soon. We met when we were freshmen in high school and were pretty much inseparable after that. He loved cooking; it was pure joy for him to make something and then share it with people. One of his specialties was chili. He was not a chili con carne purist, and included beans. That's OK with me; I drink beer and smile when making this. I use lots of chili powder, turkey stock, any extra turkey gravy, and chile butter, too. The more flavor the better.

NOTE: No leftover turkey? Use 1 lb [455 g] ground turkey and 1 lb [455 g] ground beef. Heat 1 Tbsp of olive oil in a large pot over high heat, and add the ground meat. Cook until lightly browned, about 5 minutes, breaking it up with a spoon. Set aside, and add to the chili in place of the cooked turkey.

SERVES 6

2 large poblano chiles

2 tsp cumin seeds

1 Tbsp olive oil

1½ large onions, chopped

3 celery stalks, with leaves, chopped

2 large garlic cloves, chopped

1 serrano chile, stemmed, seeded, and finely chopped

¼ cup chili powder

1 Tbsp dried Mexican oregano, preferably Oregano Indio (see Note, page 17)

1 fresh bay leaf, or 2 dried

3 cups [1 kg] crushed San Marzano tomatoes

2 cups [480 ml] turkey stock (page 178) or chicken broth

2 tsp fine sea salt

Fresh black pepper

2 lb [910 g] roast turkey, chopped

4 cups [850 g] borracho beans (page 145) or cooked kidney beans

1 bunch fresh cilantro (leaves and soft stems)

Any leftover chile butter from Tex-Mex roast turkey (page 173)

Any leftover gravy from Tex-Mex roast turkey

2 cups [200 g] grated cheddar cheese for garnish

1 cup [240 g] sour cream for garnish

Sliced green onions (green part only) for garnish

Using tongs, roast the poblano chiles over the open flame of a gas burner, turning the chiles until blackened on all sides, 1 to 2 minutes per side. Transfer to a small bowl and cover with plastic wrap; set aside to steam for 10 minutes. (Don't let them steam for too long, or they'll start to turn brown.)

Once the chiles have steamed, remove the blackened skins with your fingers and remove the stems, seeds, and veins. Chop the chiles into 1 in [2.5 cm] pieces and set aside.

Toast the cumin seeds in a small, dry skillet over medium heat, stirring frequently, until fragrant, 2 to 3 minutes. With a mortar and pestle or spice grinder, grind the cumin seeds to a coarse powder.

Heat the oil in a large heavy pot over medium-high heat. Add the onions, celery, garlic, roasted poblano chiles, serrano chile, chili powder, oregano, bay leaves, and the toasted cumin seeds. Stir to blend well, and cook until the onions are translucent, 5 minutes.

Add the tomatoes, turkey stock, salt, and 7 or 8 grinds of pepper. Bring to a boil, reduce the heat, and simmer, stirring occasionally, for 15 minutes.

Add the turkey, beans, cilantro, chile butter, and gravy and cook, stirring occasionally, for 10 minutes longer. Serve in bowls with cheddar cheese, sour cream, and green onions.

Make stock with the leftover turkey carcass from a roast turkey; it would be a shame to waste those good bones. Homemade turkey stock is easy to make and more flavorful than store-bought chicken broth; use it for soups and sauces or add a little to your sautés. I also use it for cooking turkey chili (page 176) or rice.

MAKES 8 TO 12 CUPS (2 TO 2.8 L)

1 cooked turkey carcass, meat mostly removed
and bones broken into large pieces

2 large onions, quartered

4 celery stalks, chopped

2 carrots

3 large garlic cloves, chopped

4 or 5 sprigs fresh thyme

2 sprigs fresh rosemary

1 tsp black peppercorns

Put the turkey carcass, onions, celery, carrots, garlic, thyme, rosemary, and peppercorns in a large stockpot. Add enough water to cover and bring to a boil. Lower the heat and simmer until reduced by half, 2½ to 3 hours, skimming the surface as needed.

Place a fine-mesh sieve over a large bowl. Use tongs to transfer the big bones and vegetables from the stockpot to the strainer. When only small bits remain, pour the stock through the strainer and into the bowl. If you want a clearer stock, discard the contents of your strainer, line it with a coffee filter or cheesecloth, and strain the stock again into another bowl or clean pot.

If not using immediately, pour the stock into jars or storage containers. Cool for 30 minutes, cover, and refrigerate for up to 1 week or freeze for up to 3 months.

Birria, the famous stew of Jalisco, in western Mexico, is traditionally made with goat, and sometimes beef. I love this stew; at Bar Amá we make it with braised lamb, and serve it in bowls with warm corn tortillas on the side. You can also use the meat for tacos. The lamb is cooked slowly with guajillo chiles, freshly roasted poblanos, lots of spices, and plenty of garlic, for a deeply flavorful stew.

SERVES 8 TO 10

2 poblano chiles

5 guajillo chiles, seeded, stemmed, and halved lengthwise

1 cup [240 ml] hot water

4 lb [1.8 kg] boneless lamb shoulder, cut into 1 ½ in [4 cm] cubes

1 Tbsp fine sea salt

¼ cup [60 ml] avocado or olive oil

1 medium white onion, finely chopped

3 ¼ cups [1.25 kg] crushed San Marzano tomatoes

¼ cup plus 2 Tbsp [90 ml] distilled white vinegar

6 garlic cloves

2 Tbsp grated fresh ginger

4 whole cloves

2 tsp dried Mexican oregano, preferably Oregano Indio (see Note, page 17)

2 tsp toasted sesame seeds

Fresh black pepper

½ tsp ground cumin

1 small cinnamon stick

2 bay leaves

½ cup [15 g] finely chopped fresh cilantro leaves

10 kumquats, thinly sliced, or 2 limes, quartered

Corn tortillas for serving, warmed in a skillet over medium heat (optional)

Heat the oven to 325°F [165°].

Using tongs, roast the poblano chiles over the open flame of a gas burner, turning the chiles until blackened on all sides, 1 to 2 minutes per side. Transfer to a small bowl, cover with plastic wrap, and set aside to steam for 10 minutes. Remove the blackened skins with your fingers and remove the stems, seeds, and veins. Cut into 1 in [2.5 cm] pieces and set aside.

Place a small skillet over medium heat. Flatten the guajillo chile halves on the hot skillet and toast, turning once, 10 to 15 seconds total. Put the chiles in a small bowl and add the water to rehydrate the chiles. Cover and set aside, until soft and pliable. Meanwhile, prepare the meat.

CONT'D

Season the lamb with the salt. Heat the oil in a large, ovenproof, heavy-bottom pot, such as a Dutch oven, over medium-high heat until hot and shimmering. Add the lamb and sear on all sides until well browned, about 12 minutes. If you had to do this in batches, return all of the browned lamb to the pot. Add the onion and cook until golden, 5 to 8 minutes.

Meanwhile, in a blender, purée the tomatoes, vinegar, garlic, ginger, cloves, oregano, sesame seeds, several grinds of black pepper, the cumin, the drained rehydrated guajillo chiles, and the roasted poblanos until smooth.

Pour the tomato and spice mixture into the pot with the lamb. Add the cinnamon stick and bay leaves. Cover the pot with a lid or foil and transfer to the oven. Cook until the meat is fork-tender, 1½ to 2 hours.

Remove from the oven and serve immediately in bowls with chopped cilantro and sliced kumquats or lime wedges. Warm corn tortillas would be good, too.

SUPER

NACHO

HOUR

Almost every table at Bar Amá orders at least one bowl of cheesy, gooey, molten queso—for dipping chips, or spooning into tacos or over enchiladas or fajitas for extra cheesiness. Queso is pure Tex-Mex. It's related to the chile con queso of northern Mexico, which is made with asadero or Chihuahua cheese. But the stuff I grew up with has the runny texture that you get from processed cheese. I don't knock it when it comes to queso—that texture is hard to match. But I've found that mixing other good melting cheeses with Velveeta make for a more flavorful queso. One is Brebirousse d'Argental (I know, it doesn't sound very Tex-Mex), the sheep's milk cheese from Lyon with a creamy-smooth paste, which reminds me of Velveeta, melts nearly as well in queso, and tastes delicious. Another is Briana, a semifirm cow's milk cheese from an Indiana producer that's a lot like an Alpine melting cheese.

MAKES ABOUT 2 CUPS (480 ML)

1 cup [240 ml] half-and-half

8 oz [230 g] Brebirousse d'Argental or Briana

6 oz [175 g] Velveeta, chopped

¼ cup [25 g] finely grated Monterey Jack cheese

¼ cup [25 g] finely grated cheddar cheese

Fine sea salt

Optional garnishes

Crema Mexicana

Finely chopped red onion

Thinly sliced jalapeño chile

Mexican salmorejo (page 28)

Tía Mona's picadillo (page 66)

Amá's guacamole (page 189)

Tortilla chips (page 187) for serving

Heat the half-and-half in a medium saucepan over medium-low heat until hot (not boiling). Pour it into a blender and add the Brebirousse. Blend until combined.

Return the mixture to the saucepan, raise the heat to medium, and add the Velveeta, Monterey Jack, and cheddar cheeses, melting each one before adding the next. Whisk in the salt. When all of the cheeses are melted and fully blended, transfer to a serving bowl or bowls. Put the garnishes in bowls, if using, and serve immediately with tortilla chips. Store any leftover queso in a covered container in the refrigerator for up to 3 days. Rewarm in a saucepan over medium heat before serving.

Yes, there's a vegan version of queso, and it's just as delicious! The consistency should be velvety. You want to add enough almond milk so that it flows like thick chocolate syrup from a spoon, but still sticks to a chip.

MAKES ABOUT 2 CUPS (480 ML)

2 cups [270 g] cashews

1 Tbsp avocado oil

½ onion, finely chopped

6 garlic cloves, finely chopped

2 chipotles in adobo

1½ to 2½ cups [360 to 600 ml] unsweetened almond milk

¾ cup [180 ml] tomatillo salsa (page 43)

2 tsp grated fresh turmeric, or 1 tsp ground turmeric

1 tsp fine sea salt

Finely diced red onion for garnish

Finely chopped fresh cilantro leaves for garnish

Tortilla chips (page 187) for serving

Heat the oven to 350°F [180°C]. Spread out the cashews in a single layer on a baking sheet. Roast them in the oven until golden and fragrant, shaking the pan occasionally, about 8 minutes. Remove from the oven and set aside to cool slightly.

Heat the avocado oil in a medium skillet over medium-high heat until hot and shimmering. Add the onion and garlic. Cook, stirring frequently, until lightly browned, 2 to 3 minutes. Add the cashews, chipotles, 1½ cups [360 ml] of the almond milk, the tomatillo salsa, turmeric, and salt. Stir to combine, and remove from the heat.

Pour the mixture into a blender and purée until smooth. Add more of the almond milk if necessary for a smooth consistency. You don't want it too thin, though; it's a dip. (If using as a sauce, you can thin it out a little more.) Transfer to a bowl, garnish with red onion and cilantro, and serve immediately with tortilla chips. Store any leftover cashew queso in a covered container in the refrigerator for up to 5 days. Rewarm in a saucepan over medium heat before serving.

For me, tortilla chips make or break a meal at a Mexican or Tex-Mex restaurant. I hate chips that are either too thin and dry (and taste almost baked) or too greasy. They have to be fried well, and they have to be triangles. It's not an aesthetic thing. Triangles fry better than strips, which tend to curl too much. And triangles are better for dipping. Finally, the chips should be freshly made and warm. No day-old chips.

MAKES ABOUT 10 CUPS (220 G)

Vegetable oil (such as avocado or grapeseed) or peanut oil for frying
Ten 6 in [15 cm] corn tortillas
½ tsp fine sea salt

Pour enough oil into a large heavy-bottom pot so that it comes up the sides nearly (and no more than) halfway. Heat the oil over medium-high heat to 375°F [190°C] on a deep-fry or candy thermometer.

Cut the tortillas into quarters, making sure to pull the pieces apart so they don't stick together.

Carefully add several chips at a time to the hot oil and fry until golden brown, gently stirring the chips constantly with a wire mesh skimmer or spider so they fry evenly and don't clump or stick to each other, about 1½ minutes.

Remove the chips from the oil with the skimmer and transfer to a paper towel–lined baking sheet. Repeat until all the chips have been fried and are on the baking sheet. Move them around so no oil is pooling on any of the chips. Season with the salt while still hot so the salt sticks to the chips, tossing to coat evenly. Serve immediately, or the same day.

The secret to Bar Amá's guacamole is celery. It adds a fresh and light accent to the rich avocados. The celery is grated, so the flavor is pretty subtle—you don't get a lot of celery flavor or texture like you would if you used chopped or sliced celery. This is also a pretty chunky guacamole, so just be careful not to overmix the avocados. You don't want it too smooth.

MAKES ABOUT 2 CUPS (240 G)

½ garlic clove

2 celery stalks

4 avocados

½ bunch fresh cilantro (leaves and soft stems), finely chopped

¼ red onion, finely chopped

1 serrano chile, stemmed and seeded (unless you want it really spicy)

Juice of 1 lime, plus more as needed

½ tsp fine sea salt, plus more as needed

Grate the garlic with a rasp-style grater into a large bowl. Grate the celery on the smallest holes of a box grater into the bowl. Cut the avocados in half lengthwise and remove the pits. Scoop out the avocado flesh with a spoon, being careful not to cut or tear through the skin (you don't want any of it in your guacamole). Discard the skin. Transfer the avocados to the bowl and add the cilantro, red onion, serrano, lime juice, and salt.

Mash the ingredients together with a fork, using a cut and fold motion, so that the mixture is very chunky. Taste and add more lime juice and salt, if desired. Serve immediately.

Super nachos is the dish of honor at Bar Amá's happy hour, an extravagant mound of fresh tortilla chips, plenty of queso, picadillo or chorizo, guacamole or avocado, salsa, jalapeños, green onions, and crema. The important thing to remember is to build in layers so that there are some toppings on every chip. Nobody likes a naked chip.

SERVES 4

Tortilla chips (page 187)

2 cups [480 ml] queso (page 185)

½ cup [120 g] Mexican salmorejo (page 28)

¼ cup [60 ml] tomatillo salsa (page 43), optional

1 cup [250 g] Tía Mona's picadillo (page 66) or Grandma Alice's chipotle chorizo (page 65)

2 avocados, pitted, peeled, and cut into a large dice

¼ cup [20 g] thinly sliced green onions (green part only)

3 Tbsp sliced pickled jalapeño chiles

¼ cup [60 g] crema Mexicana or sour cream

Arrange a layer of tortilla chips on a large platter. Drizzle over a little of the queso, Mexican salmorejo, and tomatillo salsa, if using. Sprinkle on some of the picadillo, avocado, green onions, and pickled jalapeño. Top with a few small dollops of the crema. Repeat until you have a mound of nachos, layered with toppings in between. Serve immediately.

Nachos *compuestas* are a different breed of nachos (Texas actually has many different kinds of nachos), usually a single layer of chips rather than a piled mound. *Compuesto* means "composed"; it's less haphazard. The toppings are spread on each chip, so that everyone definitely gets a little of everything with each bite. These aren't quite so "composed"; the ingredients are spread out in an even layer on a baking sheet, but you don't need to worry too much about placing them carefully. These are a great, easy appetizer that everybody likes to dig into.

SERVES 4 TO 6

Tortilla chips (page 187)

1½ cups [150 g] finely grated sharp cheddar cheese

1½ cups [150 g] finely grated Monterey Jack cheese

1 recipe Grandma Alice's chipotle chorizo (page 65)

⅓ cup [30 g] sliced pickled jalapeños

2½ Tbsp finely chopped red onion

3 Tbsp finely chopped fresh cilantro leaves

¼ cup [20 g] sliced green onions (green part only)

⅓ cup [80 g] crema Mexicana or sour cream

⅓ cup [80 g] Mexican salmorejo (page 28) or your favorite hot sauce

1 avocado, pitted, peeled, and cut into a large dice (optional)

Heat the oven to 375°F [190°C].

Spread half the chips on a baking sheet, and sprinkle with half the grated cheddar and Monterey Jack cheeses. Top with half the chorizo.

Repeat with a second layer of chips, cheese, and chorizo. Bake until the chips are lightly toasted and the cheese is melted, about 5 minutes. Garnish with the pickled jalapeños, onion, cilantro, green onions, crema, salmorejo, and avocado, if using. Serve immediately.

My mom worked every day, so after school my brother and I went to Nana's home (my maternal grandmother), where she'd give us a snack and then put us to work doing chores around the house. She always had eggs in the fridge, so deviled eggs and egg sandwiches (and sometimes deviled egg sandwiches) were in heavy rotation. I liked the chile heat in Nana's deviled eggs.

NOTE: Calabrian chiles are available at some gourmet markets and online; you can substitute a fresh jalapeño.

MAKES 16 DEVILED EGGS

¾ cup [150 g] chopped bacon (from ¼ in [6 mm] thick slices)

8 eggs

3 Tbsp mayonnaise

1 tsp Dijon mustard

2 Tbsp finely chopped red onion or shallot

2 Tbsp finely chopped celery

2 Tbsp finely chopped fresh cilantro leaves

1 Tbsp finely chopped oil-packed Calabrian chiles

1 tsp capers, coarsely chopped

½ tsp Amá spice mix (page 32) or chile powder (optional)

Fresh black pepper

Cook the bacon in a medium skillet over medium heat until the fat renders out and the bacon gets crispy on the edges. Transfer to a paper towel–lined plate to drain, and set aside.

Put the eggs in a single layer in a large saucepan and add enough water to cover them by 1½ in [4 cm]. Bring to a boil over high heat, cover, and turn the heat to low. Cook for 1 minute. Remove from the heat and let sit, covered, for 13 minutes. Drain the eggs and rinse them under cold running water for 1 minute.

Crack each egg shell and carefully peel the egg under cool running water. Discard the shells, and gently dry the eggs with paper towels. Cut them in half lengthwise, and transfer the yolks to a medium bowl. Put the whites on a serving platter and set aside.

Mash the yolks into a fine crumble with a fork. Add the mayonnaise, mustard, red onion, celery, 1 Tbsp of the cilantro, the chiles, and capers. Mix well.

Top each egg white half with a heaping tsp of the yolk mixture. Sprinkle each egg with the tiniest pinch of spice mix, if using, and a grind of pepper. Garnish the eggs with the chopped bacon and the remaining 1 Tbsp of cilantro. Serve immediately.

CONT'D

Cook the bacon, boil the eggs, and prepare the yolk mixture as described in the preceding recipe. Coarsely chop the egg whites and gently stir them into the yolk mixture. Add 3 Tbsp more of mayonnaise and the bacon and mix until well blended. (Or chop up any leftover deviled eggs and mix gently with the mayonnaise.) Divide the mixture among four slices of soft pain de mie bread, spreading it out evenly, and top with another slice of bread. Serve immediately.

A
M
Á

Nothing says happy hour like chicken wings. These are wrapped in banana leaves and steamed before they go into the fryer. We'll sneak hoja santa leaves in there, too; they both impart their aromatics during cooking. Even after it's been glazed with hot sauce and fried, the tender steamed meat has a subtle herbal flavor.

SERVES 6

2 ½ to 3 lb [1.2 to 1.4 kg] chicken wing pieces (24 to 32 separate drums and wings)

Fine sea salt and fresh black pepper

½ tsp ground cumin

4 large banana leaves

2 hoja santa leaves (see Note, page 21, optional)

½ cup [120 ml] soldadera's hot sauce (page 34) or your favorite hot sauce

¼ cup [60 ml] apple cider vinegar

¼ cup [60 ml] adobo sauce from canned chipotles in adobo

2 Tbsp dark brown sugar

2 tsp dried Mexican oregano, preferably Oregano Indio (see Note, page 17)

¼ cup [55 g] unsalted butter

2 to 3 cups [360 to 540 g] potato starch for dredging

Vegetable oil (such as avocado or grapeseed) or peanut oil for frying

Put the chicken wings on a baking sheet or in a large bowl and season with 1 tsp salt, several grinds of black pepper, and the cumin. Toss to coat evenly, and set aside.

Put a steamer rack inside a large pot and add 1 to 2 in [2.5 to 5 cm] of water. The surface of the water should be just underneath the basket. Bring the water to a boil over medium-high heat.

Meanwhile, put 2 of the banana leaves on a work surface so they overlap slightly. Their total surface area needs to be large enough to accommodate the chicken wings. Put a hoja santa leaf, if using, on top of the banana leaves. Put the chicken wings on top of the banana leaves. Put the remaining hoja santa leaf on top of the chicken wings. Put the remaining 2 banana leaves on top of the chicken wings so the leaves overlap, and wrap it all up like a package. Tie securely with kitchen string.

Put the package in the steamer, lower the heat to medium, and steam until the chicken is cooked through, 40 to 45 minutes.

Carefully unwrap the banana leaves, and discard them along with the hoja santa, if using. Transfer the chicken to a baking sheet or platter and refrigerate for 15 to 20 minutes (so they firm up a little and the skin gets slightly tacky before dredging).

To make the glaze, combine the hot sauce, vinegar, adobo, brown sugar, and 1 tsp salt in a small saucepan. Crumble over the oregano. Bring to a boil over medium-high heat, stirring frequently. Add the butter 1 Tbsp at a time, stirring in each addition until completely melted. Turn the heat down to low and keep warm.

CONT'D

Put the potato starch in a large bowl for the dredge and set aside.

Pour enough oil into a deep, heavy-bottom pot so that it comes 1 to 2 in [2.5 to 5 cm] up the sides. Heat the oil over medium-high heat until it reaches 365°F [185°C] on a deep-fry or candy thermometer.

Dredge and fry the chicken wings in a few batches: Toss the chicken wings in the potato starch to coat evenly. Carefully put them in the hot oil and fry until golden brown, 3 to 5 minutes. Transfer to a paper towel–lined baking sheet or platter.

Pour half the warm glaze into a large bowl. Toss the wings, a few at a time, in the hot glaze so that they're thinly coated. Transfer to a serving platter. Pour the remaining glaze into a bowl for a dipping sauce. Serve the wings immediately with extra sauce.

This is an easy sauté with lots of flavor. I love the chile flavor in combination with green onions, ginger, and peanuts. Plus a little butter. This dish is fun to eat with your hands. I think it tastes even better that way—shelling the shrimp right before you eat it is an entirely different experience from the usual knife-and-fork deal. Getting the sauce all over your fingers is the only way to go.

SERVES 4

1 lb [455 g] jumbo shrimp (16/20 count)

2 Tbsp olive oil

¼ cup [20 g] sliced green onions

3 garlic cloves, thinly sliced

1 Tbsp grated fresh ginger

½ tsp fine sea salt

Fresh black pepper

¼ cup [35 g] peanuts

½ tsp Ama's spice mix (page 32) or chile powder

½ tsp ground coriander

2 Tbsp Mexican sriracha (page 29) or store-bought sriracha

1 tsp soldadera's hot sauce (page 34), Cholula,
or another store-bought hot sauce

1 Tbsp unsalted butter

¼ cup [4 g] fresh cilantro leaves, coarsely chopped

¼ cup [4 g] fresh mint leaves, coarsely chopped

Juice of 1 lime

Leave the shells on the shrimp but make a single cut along the back of the shell with kitchen scissors. Use a paring knife to devein the shrimp. Set aside.

Heat the oil in a large skillet over medium-high heat until hot and shimmering. Add the green onions, garlic, ginger, salt, and a few grinds of pepper and cook until the aromatics are toasty (but don't burn the garlic), 1 minute.

Add the shrimp and sauté until the shrimp are just cooked through, 3 or 4 minutes. Add the peanuts and cook, stirring, so that they get toasty, 1 minute. Add the spice mix, coriander, sriracha, and hot sauce. Add the butter and stir to make a glaze. Stir in the cilantro and mint. Remove from the heat and squeeze over the lime juice. Adjust the salt to taste. Transfer to a platter and serve immediately.

CASCABEL PIMENTO CHEESE CHILES RELLENOS

Fresh poblanos are delicious, mild chiles, great for stuffing. Traditional chiles rellenos are stuffed with cheese or a combination of cheese and picadillo. At Bar Amá, the fillings vary, depending on the season or the ingredients that inspire the kitchen. Sometimes it's a mix of mushrooms and cheeses, or summer squash instead of mushrooms, or zucchini and picadillo. Here's it's gooey, melty pimento cheese, which makes this a great bar snack.

SERVES 4

1 cup [230 g] cascabel pimento cheese (page 47), at room temperature

½ cup [50 g] grated Monterey Jack cheese

½ cup [50 g] grated cheddar cheese

4 poblano chiles

3 cups [405 g] all-purpose flour

1 tsp fine sea salt

Fresh black pepper

3 eggs

Vegetable oil (such as avocado or grapeseed) or peanut oil for frying

¾ cup [190 g] Tía Mona's picadillo (page 66, optional), warmed

¼ cup [60 g] crema Mexicana or sour cream

Your favorite hot sauce for serving

In a medium bowl mix together the pimento, Monterey Jack, and cheddar cheeses. Transfer to a piping bag and set aside at room temperature.

Using tongs, roast the poblano chiles over the open flame of a gas burner, turning the chiles until blackened on all sides, 1 to 2 minutes per side. Transfer to a medium bowl and cover with plastic wrap; set aside to steam for 10 minutes. (Don't let them steam for too long, or they'll start to turn brown.) Rub off the charred skins with your fingers.

STUFF THE CHILES: Cut the tops of the chiles off, just enough to remove the stem. Cut a small opening at the tip of the piping bag and pipe some of the pimento cheese mixture into each chile (about ¼ cup [60 g], depending on the size of the chile); they should be full but not exploding with pimento cheese). Be careful not to tear them. Set the chiles on a plate and refrigerate for about 30 minutes. (This firms them up a little, makes them easier to handle, and helps keep the cheese mixture intact during dredging and frying.)

Heat the oven to 350°F [180°C]. Put a rack on a baking sheet and set aside. (You can also line the sheet with paper towels; just remember to remove them before baking.)

Put the flour in a large bowl or baking dish, and whisk in the salt and several grinds of black pepper until incorporated. Whisk together 3 eggs in a separate bowl until thoroughly scrambled.

Pour enough oil into a deep, heavy-bottom skillet or sauté pan so that it comes 1 in [2.5 cm] up the sides. Heat the oil over medium-high heat until hot—drop a little of the flour-egg mixture into the oil; if it starts to bubble right away, the oil is ready.

BATTER THE CHILES: With one hand, gently dredge a stuffed chile in the flour so it's lightly coated. With the other hand (so the first stays fairly clean and dry), dip it into the egg to coat. Toss the chile in the flour again so it's lightly coated (a little bit of clumping is OK). Put the chile in the hot oil and repeat with a second chile. Fry the chiles, two at a time, until golden brown on one side, 2 to 3 minutes. Flip them over gently (so as not to lose any cheese) and fry until golden brown on the second side, another 2 to 3 minutes. Transfer to the prepared baking sheet. Repeat with the remaining chiles.

Bake the chiles in the oven until the cheese gets really melty, 3 to 5 minutes. Transfer to a platter and top with picadillo (if using), crema, and hot sauce. Serve immediately.

When my mom made taquitos, she'd use any leftovers she had on hand—roast chicken, beans, picadillo—for the filling. My brother and I loved them because they were crunchy and hot, and we could pretend they were cigars before dipping them in hot sauce and eating them up. These taquitos are crunchy and crispy on the outside, and creamy and cheesy on the inside.

SERVES 6 (MAKES 24 TAQUITOS)

2 cups [480 ml] water

Fine sea salt

1 Tbsp unsalted butter

2 ears corn, kernels grated on the smallest holes of a box grater

¾ cup [120 g] semolina flour

¼ cup [25 g] grated cheddar cheese

¼ cup [25 g] grated Monterey Jack cheese

½ tsp fresh black pepper

¼ cup [20 g] sliced green onions (white and green parts)

Vegetable oil (such as avocado or grapeseed) or peanut oil for frying

Twenty-four 6 in [15 cm] corn tortillas

Salsa de aguacate (page 37), Amá's guacamole (page 189), tomatillo salsa (page 43), or crema Mexicana or sour cream, for garnish

Bring the water to a boil in a large saucepan over medium-high heat. Add 2 tsp salt, the butter, and grated corn, and gradually whisk in the semolina. Boil, whisking often, until thick, about 3 minutes. Remove from the heat, and set aside to cool.

In a large bowl, mix the cheddar and Monterey Jack cheeses, a pinch of salt, the pepper, and green onions. Add the semolina mixture and stir to combine.

Pour enough oil into a large, deep heavy-bottom pot to come 2 to 3 in [5 to 7.5 cm] up the sides. Heat over medium-high heat until the oil reaches 300°F [150°C] on a deep-fry or candy thermometer. Line a baking sheet with paper towels.

To soften the tortillas before filling, use tongs to quickly dip them, one at a time, into the oil, about 5 seconds on each side. Put them on the baking sheet and cover with a kitchen towel as you work, so they don't dry out.

Place about 3 Tbsp of the corn and cheese mixture on one side of a tortilla and tightly roll it over the filling into a tube. Secure with 1 or 2 toothpicks. Repeat until all of the tortillas are filled.

Raise the temperature of the oil to 375°F [190°C]. Fry the taquitos, in batches, without overcrowding the pot, until they are browned and crispy, flipping with tongs as needed to brown evenly, about 5 minutes. Place them on the lined baking sheet to drain, and sprinkle with a pinch of salt.

Transfer to a platter and serve hot with any or all of the garnishes.

These are Bar Amá's deluxe taquitos, filled with a mixture of tender lobster, cream cheese, and melted cheddar. The combination is great (it's kind of like our Tex-Mex version of lobster Thermidor on page 111). I think mild lobster and sharp cheeses are delicious together. Served with crema Mexicana or salsa de aguacate, these go fast.

MAKES 8 TAQUITOS

One 1 ½ lb [680 g] lobster

1 cup [100 g] finely grated cheddar cheese

1 cup [100 g] finely grated Monterey Jack cheese

8 oz [230 g] cream cheese

1 Tbsp chopped fresh tarragon

1 tsp dried hoja santa (see Note, page 21)

½ tsp grated lime zest

½ tsp grated lemon zest

½ tsp grated orange zest

1 tsp Amá spice mix (page 32) or chile powder

½ tsp fine sea salt

Fresh black pepper

Vegetable oil (such as avocado or grapeseed) or peanut oil for frying

Eight 6 in [15 cm] corn tortillas

Salsa de aguacate (page 37) for serving

Crema Mexicana or sour cream for serving

Prepare an ice bath by filling a large stainless steel bowl with ice water and set aside. Bring a large pot of water to a rolling boil. Add the lobster and cover. Once the water returns to a boil, cook for 9 minutes.

Transfer the lobster to the ice bath to cool, about 5 minutes. Remove from the ice bath and using kitchen shears, split the lobster shell in half lengthwise, starting from the tail. Remove the tail meat and set aside. If you have a Maine lobster, use kitchen shears to remove the top half of each claw shell, cutting along the crease of the claw (it's kind of like opening the lid of a box). Remove the claw meat and set aside with the tail meat. (Spiny lobsters don't have claws.) Discard the remaining lobster innards (you will have empty shells). Cut the meat into ½ in [12 mm] pieces. (You should have about 2 cups [370 g].)

Mix the lobster, cheeses, cream cheese, tarragon, hoja santa, citrus zests, spice mix, salt, and a few grinds of pepper in a large bowl. Adjust the salt to taste and set aside.

Pour enough oil into a large, deep heavy-bottom pot to come 2 to 3 in [5 to 7.5 cm] up the sides. Heat over medium-high heat until the oil reaches 300°F [150°C] on a deep-fry or candy thermometer. Line a baking sheet with paper towels.

To soften the tortillas before filling, use tongs to quickly dip the tortillas, one at a time, into the oil, about 5 seconds on each side. Put them on the baking sheet and cover with a kitchen towel as you work, so they don't dry out. (Alternatively, wrap the tortillas in a kitchen towel and heat in the microwave until they are soft enough to roll easily, 1 to 2 minutes.)

Spoon about 3 Tbsp of the mixture on one side of a tortilla. Roll the tortilla tightly around the filling and secure with a toothpick. Repeat until all the tortillas are filled. Line a plate with paper towels.

Raise the oil temperature to 375°F [190°C]. Working in batches of two or three at a time, carefully place the taquitos in the hot oil and fry, flipping with tongs as needed to brown evenly, until crispy and golden brown, about 5 minutes.

Using tongs, transfer the taquitos to the paper towel lined–plate to drain. Serve with salsa de aguacate and crema Mexicana for dipping.

BORRACHO BEAN DIP

Bean dip for all your party needs. The borracho beans make this dip, because they have so much flavor—chiles and other spices, herbs, and bacon. Beans mixed with cream cheese might seem like a weird combination, but the cream cheese gives the dip a smoother texture and adds a tangy flavor. Have a lot of tortilla chips on hand, or crudités, or bread. Some crema or sour cream would be good, too. And your favorite beer.

SERVES 8

2 heaping cups [455 g] drained borracho beans (page 145)

1 Tbsp Amá spice mix (page 32) or chile powder

4 oz [115 g] cream cheese, at room temperature

½ cup [120 g] Mexican salmorejo (page 28) or your favorite salsa

1 serrano chile, stemmed, seeded, and finely chopped (optional)

1 cup [100 g] grated cheddar or Monterey Jack cheese (or a mix of both)

¼ cup [20 g] sliced green onions (green part only)

Heat the oven to 350°F [180°C].

Put the beans, spice mix, and cream cheese in a food processor and pulse until smooth. Transfer to a large bowl and use a wooden spoon to mix in the salmorejo and serrano chile, if using.

Spread out the mixture in an 8 by 8 in [20 by 20 cm] baking dish, and sprinkle evenly with the cheddar. Bake just until the cheese is melted and bubbly, 15 to 20 minutes. Garnish with green onions and serve immediately.

COLD BORRACHO BEAN DIP

Bake the dip without the cheese. Cool briefly and then refrigerate for 1 hour. Spread 1 cup [240 g] of sour cream over the bean dip. Garnish with the grated cheese and green onions and serve. Leftover dip will keep in a covered container in the refrigerator for up to 3 days.

This isn't really a chalupa; it's more like a tostada. In the part of Texas where I grew up, though, it's a chalupa—a Tex-Mex mix-up. *Chalupa* is the Spanish word for "boat," which is what a Mexican chalupa resembles. It's a small fried disk of masa with a concave center, filled with a variety of toppings. But for me, a chalupa has always been a crispy flat tortilla piled high with toppings. My maternal grandmother, Nana, would make chalupas with picadillo, shredded lettuce, lots of cheddar cheese, tomatoes, onion, and Tabasco sauce. These are topped with spicy, tender short ribs.

SERVES 8

3 lb [1.4 kg] boneless beef short ribs

3 Tbsp red-eye spice (page 36)

Vegetable oil (such as avocado or grapeseed) or peanut oil for frying

Eight 6 in [15 cm] corn tortillas

Fine sea salt

2 avocados, pitted, peeled, and lightly mashed

2 heaping cups [160 g] shredded iceberg lettuce

Mexican salmorejo (page 28) or soldadera's hot sauce (page 34)

Rub the short ribs all over with the spice mix and refrigerate for at least 2 hours and up to 6 hours.

Heat the oven to 400°F [200°C]. Put a rack in a roasting pan, and put the short ribs on the rack. Roast for 20 minutes to get some good color. Lower the temperature to 300°F [150°C], cover the meat with foil, and add enough water to the pan so that it comes up the sides about ½ in [12 mm] (this helps prevent the dripping fat from burning on the bottom of the pan and adds a little moisture.) Add more water to the pan as needed during cooking. Roast until the meat is very soft to the touch and fork-tender, 2 to 3 hours. Transfer to a work surface and shred with a fork. Set aside.

To keep the fried tortillas warm in the oven, lower the oven to 250°F [120°C].

Pour enough oil into a skillet so that it comes ¼ in [6 mm] up the sides. Heat the oil over medium-high heat until hot. It should bubble when you add a tortilla. Fry the tortillas one at a time until golden brown on the first side, 30 seconds to 1 minute. Using tongs, flip and fry the other side. Make sure it's crisp; if not, the oil should be hotter. Transfer the tortilla to a paper towel–lined baking sheet and sprinkle with a little salt. If you wish, keep the baking sheet in the oven. Repeat until all of the tortillas are fried, adding oil to the pan as needed.

(Alternatively, you can bake the tortillas for the chalupas, rather than fry them. Put them on a baking sheet and bake at 350°F [180°C] until golden and crisp, about 20 minutes, rotating the pan halfway through cooking.)

Top each crispy tortilla with a little of the mashed avocado, about ¼ cup [70 g] of short rib, a heaping ¼ cup [20 g] of lettuce, and a little salmorejo. Serve immediately.

These are simple chalupas, with red rice, lettuce, cheese, and avocado—the way I usually ate them at home as a kid. The picadillo is optional.

SERVES 8

Vegetable oil (such as avocado or grapeseed) or peanut oil for frying

Eight 6 in [15 cm] corn tortillas

Fine sea salt

2 avocados, pitted, peeled, and lightly mashed

3 cups [465 g] Mom's rice (page 148) or borracho beans (page 145), or a combination

2 cups [500 g] Tía Mona's picadillo (page 66, optional)

1 cup [100 g] grated sharp cheddar cheese

4 cups [320 g] shredded iceberg lettuce

1 cup [240 ml] Mexican salmorejo (page 28)

⅓ cup [80 g] crema Mexicana or sour cream

To keep the fried tortillas warm in the oven, heat the oven to 250°F [120°C].

    Pour enough oil into a skillet so that it comes ¼ in [6 mm] up the sides. Heat the oil over medium-high heat until hot. It should bubble when you add a tortilla. One at a time, fry the tortillas until golden brown on the first side, 30 seconds to 1 minute. Using tongs, flip and fry the other side. Make sure it's crisp; if not, the oil should be hotter. Transfer the tortilla to a paper towel–lined baking sheet and sprinkle with a little salt. If you wish, keep the baking sheet in the oven to keep warm. Repeat until all of the tortillas are fried, adding oil to the pan as needed.

    (Alternatively, you can bake the tortillas for the chalupas, rather than fry them. Put them on a baking sheet and bake at 350°F [180°C] until golden and crisp, about 20 minutes, rotating the pan halfway through cooking.)

    Spread a little of the mashed avocado over each tortilla. Top with about 3 heaping Tbsp rice or beans, 2 to 3 Tbsp picadillo (if using), 2 Tbsp cheese, and ½ cup [40 g] lettuce. Garnish with the salmorejo and crema, and serve immediately.

These aren't ordinary quesadillas. They're stuffed with a lot of delicious-ness—three kinds of cheeses, including fresh stracciatella di bufala (you can also use mozzarella di bufala), which really boosts the creamy "melti-ness" factor; fresh corn; and roasted poblano chiles. The time you put into shopping for and preparing the ingredients for the filling is worth it.

SERVES 6

1 large poblano chile

1½ cups [240 g] fresh corn kernels

½ cup [35 g] thinly sliced green onions (white and green parts)

2 Tbsp finely chopped fresh cilantro leaves

2 Tbsp fresh lime juice

2 tsp olive oil

¼ tsp Amá spice mix (page 32) or chile powder

¼ tsp fine sea salt

Fresh black pepper

6 large flour tortillas, homemade (page 59) or store-bought

1 cup [100 g] finely grated Monterey Jack cheese

1 cup [100 g] finely grated aged white cheddar cheese

1 cup [270 g] stracciatella di bufala or mozzarella di bufala

1 lime, cut into wedges

¼ cup [60 g] crema Mexicana or sour cream

¼ cup [30 g] Amá's guacamole (page 189)

Your favorite hot sauce for serving

Using tongs, roast the poblano chile over the open flame of a gas burner, turning the chile until blackened on all sides, 1 to 2 minutes per side. Transfer to a small bowl and cover with plastic wrap; set aside to steam for 10 minutes. (Don't let it steam for too long, or it will start to turn brown.) Rub off the charred skin with your fingers. Remove the stem, seeds, and veins, and dice the roasted chile.

Transfer the roasted chile to a large bowl. Add the corn, green onions, cilantro, lime juice, olive oil, spice mix, salt, and a few grinds of pepper in a large bowl.

Lay the tortillas out on a work surface and spoon about ¼ cup [60 g] of filling in the center of each. Top with 2 Tbsp of the Monterey Jack cheese, 2 Tbsp of the cheddar, and 2 Tbsp of the stracciatella.

Pour a little olive oil on a paper towel and rub all over the bottom of a large skillet to grease it. Heat over medium heat. Put a filled tortilla in the skillet, and when the cheese melts, in 2 to 4 minutes, fold it in half and transfer the quesadilla to a cutting board. Repeat with the remaining tortillas, greasing the pan as needed.

Cut the quesadillas into wedges and serve immediately with lime, crema, guacamole, and hot sauce.

Fritos are a San Antonio delicacy, invented by Gustavo Olguin, who sold the recipe to the owner of a local confectionery shop for one hundred dollars during the Great Depression. That guy then created the chip empire known as Frito-Lay. Frito pie, also a San Antonio delicacy, is the stuff of rodeos—usually a bag of the cornmeal chips split open along one side and stuffed with chili and cheese. The version served at Bar Amá is layered with carne guisada, baked in a small cast-iron casserole so the cheddar topping gets warm and bubbly, and garnished with crema, onions, and cilantro. Rather than a portable snack, it's more like a sit-down meal to share.

SERVES 4

4 cups [240 g] Fritos corn chips

1 cup [260 g] carne guisada (page 63)

1 ⅓ cups [135 g] grated cheddar cheese

¼ cup [60 g] crema Mexicana or sour cream

2 Tbsp finely diced red onion

2 Tbsp finely chopped fresh cilantro leaves

Heat the oven to 350°F [180°C].

In each of 2 small baking dishes or ovenproof casseroles, layer 1 cup [60 g] of the corn chips, ¼ cup [65 g] carne guisada, and ⅓ cup [35 g] cheddar cheese. Add another layer of chips, carne guisada, and cheese. Bake in the oven until the cheese is melted, 8 to 10 minutes. Remove from the oven and top each dish with 2 Tbsp crema, 1 Tbsp onions, and 1 Tbsp cilantro. Serve immediately.

You can find what everyone calls "puffy tacos"—tacos made with souffléed masa cooked in hot oil—all over San Antonio. They're probably the city's most iconic taco, with deep-fried shells that are as light as air. I grew up with the Lopez family's version, served at Ray's Drive Inn, which to me is the originator with the best shells—the crispiest without being greasy. We make our own version at Bar Amá—puffed tacos that fry up quickly and can be filled with anything—picadillo, chorizo, beans and rice, fried potatoes, or just avocado. The fluffy, crispy shells make everything taste delicious.

NOTE: At Bar Amá, we buy fresh masa (from nixtamal) for tortillas. It's key: The freshest masa is lighter and helps the puffed tacos keep their shape. Puffed tacos made with prepackaged masa or masa harina don't work, so don't bother. Use fresh masa—available at many specialty Mexican markets or tortillerias—within twenty-four hours so that it is soft and pliable. (Keep in mind it might take practice to properly form taco shells while deep frying.)

MAKES 10 TACOS

Vegetable oil (such as avocado or grapeseed) or peanut oil for frying

14 oz [400 g] fresh masa

2 cups [500 g] Tía Mona's picadillo (page 66) or 2 avocados, sliced

½ head iceberg lettuce, cut into thin slices

¾ cup [75 g] shredded cheddar cheese

2 tomatoes, chopped

3 Tbsp finely diced onion

Line a rimmed baking sheet with paper towels.

Pour enough oil into a deep, heavy-bottom pot to come halfway up the sides. Heat the oil over medium-high heat to 375°F [190°C].

Roll the masa into 1.4 oz [40 g] balls. Transfer to a plate and cover with a clean kitchen towel to keep them from getting dry. Working one at a time, put a ball of masa between two pieces of plastic and place in a tortilla press. Press the dough into a 5 in [12 cm] circle about ¹⁄₁₆ in [2 mm] thick. As you press each round, transfer immediately to the hot oil. You have to work quickly because the masa is fragile.

Carefully lower the tortilla into the hot oil. It will sink a bit then start to float. Use a skimmer to press it down into the oil for a second, then baste the top with oil until it starts to puff with large bubbles, 10 to 15 seconds. Flip the tortilla. Use the side edge of your skimmer to lightly press an indentation down the center, roughly forming the shape of a tortilla shell, tapping the center a few times and pressing the tortilla into the oil until entirely puffed and pale golden, 20 to 30 seconds. Transfer to the prepared baking sheet. Repeat with the remaining rounds of dough; this is a press-fry-press-fry production.

Let the puffed tortillas cool for a minute or two and then fill each with a couple spoonfuls of the picadillo or a few slices of avocado, a pinch each of lettuce and cheese, a little chopped tomato, and onion. Serve immediately with your favorite hot sauce.

The first step (it's important!) to making a margarita at Bar Amá is to rim the glass with our chile salt. We make our own spice mix with a lot of dried chiles that might include: arbol, guajillo, New Mexico, chipotle, chiles negro, pasilla de Oaxaca, and cascabel. If you use a chile powder instead, just make sure you love the flavor, so you will love the margarita. As for tequila, it should be an unaged blanco, one you'd be happy to sip straight.

MAKES 1 DRINK

Amá's chile salt rim
¼ cup [75 g] fine sea salt
1 Tbsp Amá spice mix (page 32)
1 lime wedge

Ice cubes
2 oz [60 ml] tequila blanco
½ oz [15 ml] Cointreau
½ oz [15 ml] agave nectar
¾ oz [22.5 ml] fresh lime juice

FOR THE CHILE SALT RIM: Mix the salt and spice mixture in a shallow bowl. Rub a lime wedge along the rim of a rocks glass. Dip the rim of the glass into the salt-and-spice mixture to coat.

Fill the glass with ice and set aside. Combine the tequila, Cointreau, agave, and lime juice in a cocktail shaker filled with ice. Shake, and strain over the ice in the rimmed glass. Serve immediately.

219

A spicy-sweet-tart chile lime shrub really punches up this version of a margarita, named after the adult film star Nacho Vidal, who is reportedly a fan of nachos.

NOTE : Make the chile lime shrub a few days in advance.

2 oz [60 ml] tequila blanco

½ oz [15 ml] Campari

¾ oz [22.5 ml] fresh lime juice

¾ oz [22.5 ml] chile lime shrub (recipe follows)

1 Tbsp honey

Ice cubes

1 thin lime slice for garnish

Combine the tequila, Campari, lime juice, shrub, and honey in a cocktail shaker with ice. Shake, and strain into an ice-filled rocks glass. Garnish with a lime slice and serve immediately.

CHILE LIME SHRUB

MAKES ABOUT 1 CUP (240 ML)

3 limes

1 cup [240 ml] white wine vinegar

½ tsp chile flakes

Pinch of fine sea salt

½ cup [100 g] sugar

Grate the zest of the limes with a rasp-style grater and set aside. Using a sharp knife, remove and discard all of the white pith away from the limes. Chop the limes and set aside.

Combine the vinegar, chile flakes, and salt in a small saucepan and bring to a boil. Remove from the heat. Stir in the lime zest and chopped limes. Transfer to a covered container or jar with a lid and refrigerate for 3 days to meld the flavors.

Pour the unstrained mixture into a saucepan. Add the sugar and bring to a boil, stirring occasionally until the sugar is dissolved. Remove from the heat. Strain the shrub into a heat-proof jar with a lid. Cool, uncovered. Store the shrub, covered, in the refrigerator for up to 2 weeks.

Smoky mezcal, fresh pineapple juice, serrano chile, and cilantro—this is one of my favorite cocktails. The mezcal gives it some edge, and the pineapple makes it easy drinking.

NOTE : To make simple syrup, heat 1 part water and 2 parts sugar in a saucepan over medium-high heat, stirring until the sugar is dissolved. Cool before using, then refrigerate in an airtight container for up to 2 months.

MAKES 1 DRINK

1 large ice cube, plus more ice cubes for the cocktail shaker

1 slice serrano chile, seeded

5 or 6 fresh cilantro leaves

2 oz [60 ml] mezcal

1 oz [30 ml] fresh pineapple juice

¾ oz [22.5 ml] simple syrup

½ oz [15 ml] fresh lime juice

1 pineapple leaf for garnish

Put the large ice cube in an old-fashioned glass. Muddle the serrano chile with the cilantro leaves in a cocktail shaker. Add the mezcal, pineapple juice, simple syrup, lime juice, and ice cubes. Shake vigorously and strain over the large ice cube in the glass. Garnish with the pineapple leaf.

Drinking this mezcal cocktail is like being on vacation. The Jengibre Baja refreshes with its cucumber and lime juice, but it also has a bit of a sweet-spicy kick from the ginger syrup to keep things interesting. (*Jengibre* is the Spanish word for ginger.)

MAKES 1 DRINK

2 oz [60 ml] mezcal

1 oz [30 ml] cucumber juice

½ oz [15 ml] fresh lime juice

¾ oz [22.5 ml] ginger syrup (recipe follows)

Crushed ice

Combine the mezcal, cucumber juice, lime juice, and ginger syrup with ice in a cocktail shaker. Shake quickly and strain into a collins glass filled with crushed ice. Serve immediately.

GINGER SYRUP

MAKES ABOUT 2¾ CUPS (660 ML)

1 lb [455 g] fresh ginger, peeled

1½ cups [300 g] sugar

Juice the ginger with an electric juicer or juice extractor, and strain the juice into a medium saucepan. You should have about 1¼ cups [300 ml] of juice. Add the sugar and bring to a boil, stirring occasionally until the sugar has completely dissolved. Remove from the heat. Cool and store in a covered jar or container in the refrigerator for up to 5 days or in a sealed container in the freezer for up to 1 month.

A way cooler version of a Tom Collins, made with mezcal instead of gin. It's a perfect afternoon cocktail and a next-level highball: effervescent with club soda, smoky with mezcal. The orange slice is dipped in *sal de gusano*, literally "worm salt," which is made with worms traditionally found in mezcal bottles. (It's available online.)

MAKES 1 DRINK

2 oz [60 ml] mezcal

½ oz [15 ml] fresh lemon juice

¼ oz [7.5 ml] fresh lime juice

½ oz [15 ml] agave syrup

Ice cubes

Club soda for topping off

Sal de gusano (worm salt) for garnish

1 thin orange slice for garnish

Pour the mezcal, lemon juice, lime juice, and agave syrup into a cocktail shaker with ice. Shake and pour into an ice-filled collins glass. Top with soda.

Fill a small, shallow bowl with sal de gusano. Dip half the orange slice into the salt mixture. Garnish the cocktail with the orange slice and serve immediately.

A classic Negroni is one of my favorite cocktails, and the Bar Amá version made with mezcal, instead of gin, is delicious. We batch it in small kegs; stored properly, it gets better with age. This is a great cocktail to make ahead of a party, so you have it ready to pour for guests. (You can also give some away as a gift.)

NOTE : Serve the Negroni in a rocks glass with a large ice cube, and garnish with an orange twist.

MAKES ABOUT 100 OZ (3 L)

One 750 ml bottle mezcal

One 750 ml bottle of Campari

One 750 ml bottle sweet vermouth

3 cups [720 ml] water

4 ½ oz [135 ml] Damiana liqueur

Pour the mezcal, Campari, sweet vermouth, water, and Damiana into a large container and stir to combine thoroughly. Using a funnel, pour the mixture into glass bottles. Use immediately (see Note) or store, covered, in the refrigerator for up to 1 month.

A Bar Amá best-seller, *el más chingon* —the sequel to *el chingon* (which translates as "the fucking great")—combines spicy and floral flavors. Fresh Fresno chiles are muddled with agave nectar and shaken with gin, elderflower liqueur, and citrus for a balanced drink.

MAKES 1 DRINK

3 Fresno chile slices
½ oz [15 ml] agave nectar
1½ oz [45 ml] gin
¾ oz [22.5 ml] St-Germain elderflower liqueur
½ oz [15 ml] fresh lemon juice
½ oz [15 ml] fresh lime juice
Ice cubes, plus crushed ice

In a cocktail shaker, muddle two of the chile slices with the agave nectar. Add the gin, elderflower liqueur, lemon juice, lime juice, and ice cubes. Shake quickly and vigorously. Strain into a highball glass filled with crushed ice. Garnish with the remaining slice of chile, and serve immediately.

Named for the color of the hibiscus syrup, the snake's blood cocktail is deep red and delicious. It's simultaneously rich from the rye whiskey and sweet-tart from a syrup made with dried hibiscus flowers.

MAKES 1 DRINK

1 large ice cube, plus more ice cubes for the cocktail shaker

1 ½ oz [45 ml] rye whiskey

1 oz [30 ml] Aperol

¾ oz [22.5 ml] hibiscus syrup (recipe follows)

¾ oz [22.5 ml] fresh lemon juice

1 dried hibiscus flower for garnish

Put the large ice cube into a chilled rocks glass. Pour the rye, Aperol, hibiscus syrup, and lemon juice into a cocktail shaker with ice. Shake vigorously and strain over the large ice cube in the rocks glass. Serve immediately, garnished with the dried hibiscus flower.

HIBISCUS SYRUP

MAKES ABOUT 1¾ CUPS (420 ML)

1 ½ cups [360 ml] water

2 Tbsp dried hibiscus flowers

¼ cup plus 2 Tbsp [75 g] sugar

Combine the water, hibiscus flowers, and sugar in a small saucepan and bring to a boil, stirring occasionally to dissolve the sugar. Lower the heat to medium-low and reduce the mixture by about a third. Strain into a heat-proof jar and discard the solids. Cool the syrup, and store, covered, in the refrigerator for up to 1 month.

Tart, salty, savory, refreshing michelada—the magical beer cocktail of Mexico made with some combination of hot sauce, lime, Worcestershire sauce, soy sauce, maybe Maggi seasoning, and Clamato—is the best beer-based cocktail I know. At Bar Amá, we make ours with a base of *sangrita*, or "little blood," a drink in its own right, which is traditionally partnered with a shot of tequila but is also delicious in a Michelada. The sangrita has hot sauce, adobo sauce, habanero chile, and horseradish for plenty of spice; vinegar for acid; and Worcestershire, celery salt, and Clamato for umami. Our michelada is prepared with a large hot sauce ice cube, so the drink doesn't get diluted.

NOTE : Prepare the hot sauce ice cubes the day before.

SERVES 1

Hot sauce ice cube
Soldadera's hot sauce (page 34) or your favorite hot sauce

1 ½ oz [45 ml] sangrita (recipe follows)
12 oz [360 ml] Mexican lager, such as Pacifico

MAKE THE HOT SAUCE ICE CUBE: For each drink that you plan to make, pour 2 Tbsp hot sauce into the bottom of each 2 ¼ in [5.5 cm] square ice cube mold in the tray. Fill the remainder of the mold with water, and freeze for at least 4 hours or overnight.

Put 1 hot sauce ice cube into a 1 pt [480 ml] glass. Pour in the sangrita and top with beer. Serve immediately.

SANGRITA

MAKES ABOUT 2½ CUPS (600 ML)

2 cups [480 ml] Clamato
3 Tbsp soldadera's hot sauce (page 34) or your favorite hot sauce
2 Tbsp red wine vinegar
2 Tbsp prepared horseradish
2 Tbsp adobo sauce from canned chipotles in adobo
1 tsp Worcestershire sauce
1 tsp celery salt
¾ tsp fine sea salt
½ tsp Amá spice mix (page 32) or chile powder
1 habanero chile, stemmed, seeded, and finely chopped

Blend all the ingredients in a blender until smooth. Store the leftover sangrita in a covered container in the refrigerator for up to 5 days.

CES

& DESSERTS

A big bowl of berries is one of my favorite summer desserts to set out on the dinner table. Toss the berries with torn mint and drizzle with a hibiscus-ginger syrup. The syrup adds another layer of flavor—sweet and tart, floral and fruity—to a simple dish. It's also great to have around for cocktails with whiskey or mezcal or for lemonade.

SERVES 4

1 pt [240 g] blackberries

1 pt [280 g] blueberries

1 pt [240 g] raspberries

3 or 4 fresh mint leaves, torn

¼ cup [60 ml] hibiscus-ginger syrup (recipe follows)

Put the berries in a large bowl and gently toss with the torn mint. Drizzle with the hibiscus-ginger syrup and gently mix with a rubber spatula or wooden spoon. Serve immediately.

HIBISCUS-GINGER SYRUP

MAKES ABOUT 3 CUPS (720 ML)

2 cups [480 ml] water

1 cup [200 g] sugar

½ cup [20 g] dried hibiscus flowers

2 tsp grated fresh ginger

Pinch of fine sea salt

1 tsp key lime juice

¼ vanilla pod

Combine the water, sugar, hibiscus flowers, ginger, and salt in a large saucepan. Bring to a boil over medium-high heat, stirring occasionally to make sure the sugar dissolves. Remove from the heat and add the lime juice. Scrape the vanilla seeds and add them, along with the pod, to the pot. Let sit for 10 to 15 minutes. Strain the syrup through a fine-mesh sieve and set aside to cool. When cool, set aside ¼ cup [60 ml] for the berries. Store the leftover syrup in a covered container in the refrigerator for up to 2 weeks.

This is a super easy recipe for *flan de queso*, "cheese flan," made with cream cheese, evaporated milk, and sweetened condensed milk. You don't need any additional sugar, because the condensed milk makes it just sweet enough. At Bar Amá, we bake these in individual dishes, so there's no need to unmold them. And instead of a layer of caramel, it's topped with sliced blood oranges and a sprinkle of sugar caramelized with a cooking torch into a golden, crackly crust.

SERVES 6

4 oz [115 g] cream cheese, at room temperature

4 eggs plus 3 egg yolks

¾ cup [180 ml] sweetened condensed milk

¾ cup [180 ml] evaporated milk

1 tsp vanilla extract

Seeds of ½ vanilla pod

½ tsp grated blood orange zest, plus 2 blood oranges, thinly sliced

Pinch of fine sea salt

6 Tbsp [90 g] sugar

Heat the oven to 325°F [165°C].

Put the cream cheese, eggs, egg yolks, condensed milk, evaporated milk, vanilla extract and seeds, blood orange zest, and salt in a blender. Blend until smooth, about 1 minute. Strain the mixture through a fine-mesh sieve. (This makes a generous 3 cups [720 ml] of custard.)

Set six baking dishes in a roasting pan. We use 6 oz [180 ml] ovenproof bowls, but you can use any size of ramekin or individual baking dish. Pour the custard into the ramekins, dividing it evenly among them. Carefully pour hot water into the roasting pan so that it comes halfway up the sides of the ramekins.

Bake until the custards are set but still jiggly in the center; start checking at 20 minutes, and every 5 minutes after (the timing will depend on the size of your ramekins and how much you've filled them). Remove from the oven and let cool slightly in the water. Remove from the water and cover lightly with plastic wrap. Chill in the refrigerator for at least 2 hours or overnight to set.

Remove the custards from the refrigerator. Top each with 2 or 3 slices of blood orange and 1 Tbsp sugar. Caramelize the tops with a cooking torch. Serve immediately.

BRISKET AND COBBLER

The Miller sisters were better known for their smoked brisket than for their cobbler. But my family rarely ordered one without the other. It was usually for a special occasion, like Christmas—because we considered Christmas barbecue an appropriate holiday dinner.

Myrtle, Bernice, and Ethel ran Miller's Bar B Q in the backyard of what was originally their parents' San Antonio home. My family didn't barbecue like the Millers barbecued. For the most part, we hewed to get-it-hot-and-cook-it-fast methods, ranchero style. So we counted on the Millers for brisket and big beef ribs known as beef back ribs, with plenty of meat between the bones. Later on, toward the end of the Millers' fifty-year run, they would smoke an occasional turkey or duck, just for my dad.

Three generations of the Centenos ate at the Millers', not far from where the first Centeno Super Market opened on the West Side. Myrtle, Bernice, and Ethel's parents opened the family smoke shack after their father, Harvey Miller, retired from his job with the railroad in 1941. He, like my Mama Grande, was from Floresville. San Antonio wasn't known for its barbecue, but a lot of nearby central Texas towns are worth driving to for smoked meats—such as New Braunfels, Floresville, and Lockhart. The whole Miller family knew their low 'n' slow. Eventually, the three sisters took over the business.

You'd have to walk around their house to a small smoke shack in the back supported by bricks and surrounded by metal screens for ventilation. A hand-painted sign said "Millers' Bar B Q" above a Coca-Cola logo, and a metal plate on the screen door said "ButterKrust Bread." Along with brisket and beef ribs, the Millers served country rings of Polish sausage, sandwiches, beans, and potato salad. Fruit cobbler was the only sweet.

In the middle of the smoke shack was a pit with a two-level metal grill, covered with decades of char by the time I started eating there. They probably smoked nearly 150 lb [68 kg] of ribs at a time with oak wood, all night. It was so smoky inside you could barely open your eyes. There were a handful of tables inside, but most took their barbecue home or ate out in the yard.

It was a homey institution that was also probably barely legal. A pamphlet printed when the Millers eventually closed shop quotes Myrtle: "My inspector told me he would never give me a citation, he told me he'd give me a petition saying I couldn't close up, I meant too much to the city of San Antonio. We never had a complaint about the food. Our place was small and in the backyard of our home. We served all colors, and we never had a fight. We didn't have beer, so there were no bottles thrown, and the only music was the cracking of the bones and the chewing of the barbeque."

Myrtle and my dad met for the first time in the parking lot of the Centeno market when she pulled up in her old Lincoln. Grandma Alice was a customer of the Millers', and Myrtle sought out my dad to ask him for a donation for one of her church events—a case of wine and some food, which he ended up delivering to her personally. So from then on he was in with Myrtle. He continued to deliver groceries to her, and when we needed a home for one of our dogs, Sadie, Myrtle took her in.

Eventually Dad was privy to the kitchen in the Millers' house, where they made their secret barbecue sauce right in front of him, with brown sugar, ketchup, vinegar, and Worcestershire sauce, as he recalls it. My dad replicated it the best he could, and we make a version of his at Bar Amá.

But I'd sooner forgo barbecue sauce with my brisket than cobbler. The cobbler always came in a large tin pan, a golden crust of flaky dough baked over soft peaches. When it was scooped onto a plate, the crust would break up and get mixed with the warm fruit. Everybody remembers it as "the best cobbler ever," and it's probably why cobbler is my favorite dessert—even though I make a biscuit-topped version.

Funnel cakes are plentiful at fairs in south and central Texas. They're made by pouring cake batter through a funnel into hot oil in a circular pattern. When golden brown, they're sprinkled with powdered sugar and eaten hot. At Bar Amá, we make our dough like the choux pastry used for cream puffs and churros, so they're extra light and airy.

MAKES 8 FUNNEL CAKES

Chocolate sauce

1 cup [240 ml] heavy cream

1 cup [240 ml] agave syrup

1 wedge Ibarra chocolate, chopped

2 cups [295 g] coarsely chopped bittersweet chocolate

Funnel cakes

¾ cup [165 g] unsalted butter, cut into pieces

2 Tbsp sugar

¼ tsp fine sea salt

2 cups [270 g] all-purpose flour

8 eggs plus 4 egg whites

Vegetable oil (such as avocado or grapeseed) or peanut oil for frying

Powdered sugar for garnish

Vanilla bean semifreddo (page 252) for serving

MAKE THE CHOCOLATE SAUCE: In a medium saucepan, heat the cream, agave syrup, and Ibarra chocolate over medium heat, stirring frequently, until the chocolate is completely dissolved. Remove from the heat, add the bittersweet chocolate, and stir until melted and the sauce is smooth. It's ready to use. Store leftover sauce in a covered container in the refrigerator for up to 5 days. Rewarm over medium heat before serving.

MAKE THE FUNNEL CAKES: Combine the butter, sugar, and salt in a medium heavy-bottom pot over medium-high heat. When the butter is melted and sizzling, add the flour and stir vigorously with a wooden spoon until the dough pulls together into a stiff mass and pulls away from the sides of the pot.

Transfer the dough to the bowl of a stand mixer fitted with the paddle attachment and mix on medium speed until warm or at room temperature to the touch. You don't want it too hot, or it will cook the eggs in the next step.

CONT'D

Add the eggs and egg whites, one a time, and continue to mix, making sure each is fully incorporated before adding the next. Transfer the dough to a piping bag fitted with a 7⁄16 in [11 mm] round tip and set aside.

Fill a heavy-bottom pot with oil so that it comes nearly halfway up the sides. Heat the oil over medium-high heat to 375°F [190°C] on a deep-fry or candy thermometer. Carefully pipe the dough into the oil in a zigzag and swirl pattern, creating a disk of squiggles about 5 in [12 cm] across. Fry until golden brown, about 3 minutes per side, flipping once. Using a skimmer, transfer the funnel cake to a paper towel–lined baking sheet to drain. Repeat with the remaining batter.

Put each funnel cake in a shallow bowl or on a plate and sprinkle with powdered sugar. Serve immediately with vanilla bean semifreddo and chocolate sauce.

I love cobbler because it's so simple—fruit baked with a golden, buttery topping. Texas-style cobbler is covered with cake, but I grew up eating a lot of pielike cobbler with a flaky crust. Now I make mine with biscuits, the classic topping outside of Texas. The biscuits are golden, flaky, tender, and crunchy, all at once. And the fruit—always seasonal—gets jammy and bubbly. It's always delicious with ice cream.

SERVES 8

⅓ to ½ cup [65 to 100 g] sugar (depending on the sweetness of your berries)

2 Tbsp all-purpose flour or cornstarch

6 cups [840 g] blueberries, or a combination of blueberries, blackberries, and mulberries

2 Tbsp hibiscus-ginger syrup (page 237, optional)

½ recipe biscuit dough (page 73), refrigerated and then rolled out

Ice cream for serving (optional)

Whisk together the sugar and flour in a large bowl. Add the berries and hibiscus-ginger syrup, if using, and toss to coat the berries. Transfer the berries to a 9 or 10 in [23 or 25 cm] round cake pan or baking dish and set aside to macerate for about 20 minutes.

Heat the oven to 350°F [180°C].

Tear the biscuit dough into 1 or 2 in [2.5 to 5 cm] pieces, or any size you like. (They don't all have to be the same size.) Arrange the biscuit pieces in a single layer on top of the berry mixture, about ½ in [12 mm] apart.

Bake until the berries are bubbling and the biscuit topping is golden brown, about 55 minutes. Remove from the oven and set aside to cool slightly. Serve with ice cream, if you like.

These sopapillas are made with flour tortilla dough, which has a little bit of leavening in it and puffs up when fried. The sopapillas are rolled smaller than tortillas and slightly thicker. While frying, they bubble and fill with air—and happiness.

MAKES 8 SOPAPILLAS

½ cup [100 g] sugar

1 tsp ground cinnamon

1 recipe flour tortilla dough from Tía Carmen's flour tortillas (page 59)

Vegetable oil (such as avocado or grapeseed) or peanut oil for frying

Honey for garnish

Combine the sugar and cinnamon in a small bowl, and set aside.

Lightly flour a work surface. Divide the flour tortilla dough into eight 1 oz [30 g] balls and roll out each one into a disk about 3½ in [9 cm] round and ⅛ in [4 mm] thick.

Pour enough oil into a heavy-bottom skillet or pot so that it comes 2 in [5 cm] up the sides. Heat the oil over medium-high heat to 375°F [190°C] on a deep-fry or candy thermometer.

Fry a few of the sopapillas at a time, raising or lowering the heat as needed to maintain the temperature of the oil. As the sopapillas puff up and rise to the surface, baste the tops of the sopapillas with oil with a long-handled spoon. Fry until golden brown, 1 to 2 minutes on each side, flipping once. Carefully remove the sopapillas from the oil with a slotted spoon and drain on several layers of paper towels or a brown paper bag. Cool slightly. Sprinkle with cinnamon sugar and drizzle with honey. Serve immediately.

These are the *conchas*, shell-shaped sweet breads, that we make at Bar Amá on weekends for brunch. They're fluffy and just sweet enough, with a crunchy layer of streusel dough baked on top. I especially like these because they have lots of flavor, thanks to the cinnamon, fennel, clove, and orange zest. And freshly made is one hundred times better than any store-bought.

MAKES 15 CONCHAS

Concha dough

½ cup plus 2 Tbsp [140 g] unsalted butter

4 ¼ cups [575 g] all-purpose flour

2 ½ tsp salt

¼ tsp ground cinnamon

¼ tsp ground clove

¼ tsp ground fennel

1 tsp grated orange zest

⅓ cup plus 2 Tbsp [95 g] sugar

One ¾ oz [20 g] packet active dry yeast

¾ cup plus 2 tsp [190 ml] milk

1 egg

Streusel paste

½ cup [110 g] unsalted butter

½ cup [60 g] powdered sugar

½ cup [70 g] all-purpose flour

½ tsp vanilla extract

MAKE THE CONCHA DOUGH: Take the butter out of the refrigerator about 20 minutes before you start to make the dough; it should be pliable, but still cool. Cut into ½ in [12 mm] pieces and set aside.

Whisk together the flour, salt, cinnamon, clove, fennel, and orange zest in a medium bowl and set aside. Put half of the sugar and all of the yeast in the bowl of a stand mixer fitted with a dough hook and set aside.

Heat the milk with the remaining sugar in a small saucepan over medium-low just until warm. Pour the warm milk over the yeast, stir, and let it sit until the yeast is active and foamy, about 10 minutes.

With the mixer running, slowly start adding the flour a little at a time. Continue mixing and increase the speed to medium-high until it is a smooth, elastic dough, about 3 minutes, scraping the sides of the bowl as needed. Add the butter a little at a time, making sure each addition is fully incorporated before adding more. The dough will form a mass around the dough hook and pull away from the sides of the bowl.

Transfer the dough to a lightly floured surface and shape it into a ball. Spray a large bowl with cooking spray. Put the dough in the bowl and cover with plastic wrap. Let it rise in a warm place until the dough has doubled in size, about 1½ hours.

Meanwhile, make the streusel paste: In the bowl of the stand mixer fitted with the paddle attachment, beat the butter on medium speed until smooth. Reduce the speed to low and slowly pour in the powdered sugar and flour. Mix until fully incorporated. Add the vanilla and mix until smooth. Wrap the mixture in plastic and refrigerate for at least 20 minutes while you shape the concha dough.

Line two baking sheets with parchment paper. When the dough has doubled in size, transfer it to a lightly floured surface. Divide the dough into fifteen pieces. Form the pieces into balls by cupping your lightly floured palm over a ball of dough and rolling in a circular motion while pressing gently against the ball. Transfer the dough balls to the prepared baking sheet, spacing evenly. Set aside.

On a lightly floured surface, roll out the streusel paste to a thickness of ⅛ in [4 mm]. Use a 4 in [10 cm] circular cutter to cut out circles, and carefully place them over the dough balls. Using a sharp paring knife, score the top with parallel lines, starting ¾ in [2 cm] from one edge and stopping ¾ in [2 cm] from the other. Cut just through the streusel layer to create the traditional shell pattern. Cover with a clean kitchen towel and set aside until doubled in size, about 1 hour.

Heat the oven to 350°F [180°C]. Bake until golden brown, 25 to 30 minutes, rotating the baking sheet halfway through. Serve warm or at room temperature. These are best the day they're baked.

Kikuko Hallock (Betty's mom) was born in Tokyo, and it wasn't until she moved to the United States in her thirties that she learned to make pecan pie (a Texas classic!) from reading cookbooks and then tweaking and tweaking. This is a not-too-sweet pecan pie, with crunchy nuts and a crisp, flaky crust. She developed some quirky techniques over the years, but it's the best pecan pie I've ever had—so her techniques must work. She serves it without whipped cream, without ice cream. It's perfect as is.

NOTE : To make sure all of the ingredients for the pie crust are very cold, refrigerate them the night before baking. Mama Hallock uses only metal (aluminum) pie tins.

MAKES ONE 9 IN PIE

Single crust pie dough
1 ⅓ cups [185 g] all-purpose flour
½ tsp salt
½ cup [110 g] unsalted butter, cut into small pieces
3 ½ Tbsp [50 ml] cold water

Filling
3 eggs
1 egg yolk
⅓ cup [65 g] lightly packed dark brown sugar
⅓ cup [65 g] granulated sugar
¼ tsp salt
2 tsp cornstarch
¼ cup [60 ml] melted unsalted butter, cooled
1 generous cup [250 ml] dark corn syrup
1 tsp vanilla extract
1 ½ heaping cups [185 g] pecans halves

The day before you make the pie, sift the flour with the salt and put the mixture, as well as the butter pieces, in the refrigerator. Place a mixing bowl in the freezer overnight, too.

MAKE THE DOUGH: Put the flour and salt mixture in the cold bowl and add the butter. With a pastry cutter, cut the butter into the flour, turning the bowl as you're cutting, until the mixture is crumbly (fine crumbs).

Before adding the cold water, visualize the mixture in the bowl as four quadrants. Add 1 scant Tbsp of cold water to the first quadrant and mix, using a fork, until incorporated. Repeat for the next three quadrants. Give the whole mixture a final mix with the fork. Using your hands, gather the dough into a smooth ball. Flatten it into a disk, wrap with plastic, and refrigerate for at least 15 minutes and up to overnight.

Place a 13 in [33 cm] piece of wax paper on your work surface. Place the unwrapped pie crust on top of the wax paper. Sprinkle it lightly with flour. Roll from the center out, rotating the wax paper, to form a rough circle of dough 11 in [28 cm] in diameter. Transfer the dough to your pie pan by inverting the wax paper over the pan. Gently pat the dough into the corners of the pan. Refrigerate for at least 15 minutes to relax the gluten.

Fold the overhanging dough underneath itself, and press gently all the way around to make it flush with the edge of the pie pan. Fill a small bowl with cold water. Dip your thumb and forefinger into the water and crimp the dough all the way around. Reapply water to the crimped crust edges, going all the way around. Re-dip your thumb and forefinger into the water as needed.

Arrange an oven shelf so that it's on the lowest position of the oven. Preheat the oven to 425°F [220°C].

MAKE THE FILLING: Put the three eggs and the yolk in a mixing bowl, beating each egg with a whisk before the addition of the next. Set a small strainer over another bowl. Strain the egg mixture, pushing the beaten eggs through with a rubber spatula. (This makes a smoother custard.)

Add both sugars and the salt, and beat the mixture well with a whisk until well incorporated.

In a separate small bowl, mix the cornstarch into the melted butter, using a small spoon, until completely smooth. Add that mixture to the egg-sugar mixture. Beat well with a whisk. Add the dark corn syrup and beat well. Add the vanilla extract and mix well. Then stir in the pecans.

Put the prepared pie crust on a baking sheet. Pour the filling into the crust. Put the pie on the bottom rack of the oven. Bake for 15 minutes, then reduce the heat to 375°F [190°C] and bake for an additional 20 minutes. Reduce the heat to 350°F [180°C] and bake for another 20 minutes. Cover lightly with foil for the last 10 minutes to prevent the edges of the crust from getting too dark. Check the pie for doneness: A knife inserted halfway between the center of the pie and the edge will come out clean.

Cool completely to set the filling, about 1 hour, on a rack. Store the pie, covered with foil, for up to 3 days in a cool place or in the refrigerator.

This is an easy version of vanilla ice cream, which we make at Bar Amá with cream and crème fraîche—no ice-cream maker necessary! We use it for *raspados* of shaved ice and hibiscus syrup, for fried ice cream, or to serve drizzled with dulce de leche or chocolate sauce.

SERVES 6 TO 8

Vanilla bean semifreddo
6 egg yolks
1½ tsp dark brown sugar
½ cup [100 g] granulated sugar
1½ cups [360 ml] heavy cream
½ cup [120 g] crème fraîche
Seeds of 1 vanilla bean

Dulce de leche
One 14 oz [420 ml] can sweetened condensed milk

MAKE THE SEMIFREDDO: Put the egg yolks, brown sugar, and granulated sugar in the bowl of a stand mixer fitted with the whisk attachment. Mix on medium-high to high speed until the mixture is pale yellow and fluffy, about 8 minutes. Set aside.

Combine the heavy cream, crème fraîche, and vanilla seeds scraped from the bean in a clean bowl, and with a clean whisk attachment, or a hand mixer with regular beaters, whip until soft peaks form.

Carefully fold the whipped cream mixture into the egg mixture. Pour into a container, cover, and freeze for 6 hours or overnight. Any leftover ice cream will keep in the freezer for up to 1 week.

MAKE THE DULCE DE LECHE: Peel the label off the can of condensed milk and put the can in a large pot. Add enough water to the pot so it comes within 2 fingers of the top. Bring to a boil over medium-high heat. Lower the heat to medium-low and cook for 6 hours, checking the water level, and adding more as needed to keep the pot filled. Remove the can with tongs and set aside to cool overnight at room temperature.

Serve the semifreddo with a drizzle of the dulce de leche. Store any remaining dulce de leche in a covered container in the refrigerator for up to 1 month.

I'm pretty sure that fried ice cream has been on every menu of every sit-down Tex-Mex restaurant I've been to. Frying ice cream seems implausible, but once coated in cornflake crumbs and refrozen, it's no problem. The balls of ice cream fry up nicely. Just make sure to refreeze the scoops of ice cream until very firm after coating them.

SERVES 8

1 recipe vanilla bean semifreddo (page 252) or vanilla ice cream

3 cups finely crushed cornflakes or graham crackers

1 tsp ground cinnamon

3 egg whites

Vegetable oil (such as avocado or grapeseed) or peanut oil for frying

Dulce de leche (page 252) or chocolate sauce (page 241) for serving (optional)

Whipped cream for serving (optional)

Let the semifreddo sit out until just soft enough to scoop easily. Using a 3 oz [85 g] scoop, scoop eight balls of semifreddo onto a baking sheet and freeze for 1 hour or until firm.

In a shallow dish, combine the cornflake crumbs and cinnamon. In another shallow dish, beat the egg whites until foamy. Roll the semifreddo balls in the egg whites, and then in the cornflake crumbs. They should be covered completely with crumbs; repeat if necessary. Freeze them again until firm, at least 3 hours, or if you're making these in advance, up to 1 week, covered.

Fill a heavy-bottom pot with oil so that it comes nearly halfway up the sides. Heat the oil over medium-high heat to 375°F [190°C] on a deep-fry or candy thermometer. Using a slotted spoon, lower one or two semifreddo balls into the oil and fry until golden, 10 to 15 seconds. Drain quickly on paper towels, and repeat with the remaining semifreddo balls, raising or lowering the heat to maintain the temperature of the oil. Serve immediately, with dulce de leche and whipped cream, if desired.

A riff on a classic French cookie, these are thin and delicious, with a lot of texture from cacao nibs, shredded dried coconut, and toasty pecans (a Texas favorite). They are barely sweet, great for snacking or enjoying as a dessert with a glass of dry sherry.

¾ cup plus 1 ½ Tbsp [105 g] toasted pecans

1 ¾ cups [245 g] all-purpose flour

¼ cup [30 g] powdered sugar

½ tsp fine sea salt

Scant 1 cup [200 g] cold unsalted butter, cubed

1 egg white

1 Tbsp coconut cream

¼ cup [20 g] unsweetened shredded coconut

3 Tbsp cacao nibs

Put the pecans in a food processor and pulse a few times until ground (not too coarse, and not too fine). Add the flour, powdered sugar, and salt and pulse to combine. Add the butter and pulse until the dough is crumbly. Add the egg white and coconut cream and pulse just until incorporated.

Transfer the dough to a large mixing bowl. Using a rubber spatula or your hands, fold in the shredded coconut and cacao nibs. Form the dough into a disk, wrap with plastic, and refrigerate for at least 1 hour and up to 2 days.

Heat the oven to 350°F [180°C]. Line 2 baking sheets with parchment paper and set aside.

Transfer the dough to a lightly floured work surface and roll it out until ¼ in [6 mm] thick. With a 2 ½ in [6 cm] round cookie cutter, cut out as many cookies as you can. You can reroll the dough scraps and cut out more.

Place the cookies on the prepared baking sheets at least ½ in [12 mm] apart and bake until the edges are lightly browned, 15 to 20 minutes. Remove from the oven and cool completely on a rack. Store the cookies in a covered container for up to 1 week.

The cake of choice for every tía's birthday party was tres leches—sponge cake soaked in a sweet mixture of three milks: condensed milk, evaporated milk, and heavy cream. I like Bar Amá's version because it switches up the flavors and isn't too sweet, but is also super moist. The cake provides a fluffy chocolaty base for the soaking liquid, made with coconut milk, cream, and coffee (our three "milks"). The cream cheese frosting with a sprinkling of chocolate cookie crumbs takes it over the top. This recipe makes more chocolate graham crumbs then you will need for the cake. Store extra in a sealed bag or airtight container in the freezer for up to 3 months.

259

SERVES 12 TO 15
(MAKES ONE 9 BY 13 IN [23 BY 33 CM] CAKE)

Chocolate cake

1 ¾ cups [245 g] all-purpose flour

1 Tbsp plus 1 tsp baking powder

1 ½ cups [300 g] sugar

¾ cup [60 g] cocoa powder

¾ cup [180 ml] whole milk

1 ½ tsp vanilla extract

7 eggs, separated

Chocolate graham crumbs

2 ½ cups [300 g] graham crumbs

1 cup [240 ml] heavy cream

¼ cup [55 g] unsalted butter, melted

¼ cup [20 g] cocoa powder

¼ cup [50 g] sugar

½ tsp fine sea salt

Coco-coffee milk

2 cups [240 ml] coconut milk

2 cups [480 ml] heavy cream

½ cup [120 ml] coffee

½ cup [100 g] sugar

Cream cheese frosting

1 lb [455 g] cream cheese, at room temperature

1 ½ cups [330 g] unsalted butter, at room temperature

½ cup [60 g] powdered sugar

CONT'D

MAKE THE CHOCOLATE CAKE: Heat the oven to 350°F [180°C]. Butter a 9 by 13 in [23 by 33 cm] cake pan and line it with parchment paper; set aside.

Sift the flour and baking powder into a bowl and set aside. In a medium bowl, whisk together the sugar, cocoa powder, milk, and vanilla until well blended. Set aside.

Pour the egg whites into the bowl of a stand mixer fitted with a whisk attachment and whip on medium-high speed until the egg whites form stiff peaks. Remove the bowl from the mixer. In a medium bowl, whisk the egg yolks by hand until fluffy. Fold the egg yolks into the whites until lighter and lemon colored. Fold in the cocoa mixture next, and then the flour mixture.

Pour the cake batter into the prepared pan and bake until a tester inserted in the cake comes out clean, 50 minutes to 1 hour. Cool completely.

MAKE THE CHOCOLATE GRAHAM CRUMBS: Leave the oven at 350°F [180°C]. Line a baking sheet with parchment paper and set aside. With a wooden spoon, mix the graham crumbs, cream, melted butter, cocoa powder, sugar, and salt in a large bowl. Spread out the mixture in an even layer on the prepared baking sheet and bake until the texture of dry sand, 10 to 15 minutes. Remove from the oven and cool slightly. Blend in a food processor or blender until it resembles a coarse powder. (The crumbs can be made up to 5 days in advance and stored in a covered container.)

MAKE THE COCO-COFFEE MILK: Combine the coconut milk, cream, coffee, and sugar in a blender and blend until the sugar has dissolved. Refrigerate until ready to use.

MAKE THE CREAM CHEESE FROSTING: Put the cream cheese, butter, and powdered sugar in the bowl of a stand mixer fitted with the paddle attachment. Cream the ingredients, gradually increasing the speed to medium-high, until the frosting is fluffy and airy, 4 to 6 minutes.

When the cake has cooled, pour the coco-coffee milk over the top to soak the cake thoroughly. Frost the top with the cream cheese frosting, and sprinkle with the chocolate graham crumbs. Serve immediately. Store left-over cake, well covered, in the refrigerator for up to 2 days.

Capirotada is the traditional Mexican bread pudding served at Lent. Each of the ingredients in the pudding has some religious meaning, and they also happen to be delicious together. Spices, raisins, nuts, coconut, bananas, sugar, and cream go into a custard, which is poured over torn pieces of bolillo, a Mexican bread. Serve warm with a little whipped cream.

SERVES 12

½ cone (4 ½ oz [125 g]) piloncillo (see Note, page 58)

1 cup [240 ml] water

10 day-old bolillos or baguettes, torn into bite-size pieces

1 cup [150 g] golden raisins

1 cup [150 g] roasted peanuts

1 cup [85 g] toasted shredded coconut

1 cup [140 g] crumbled queso fresco

2 ripe bananas, chopped

4 cups [960 ml] heavy cream

2 cups [480 ml] milk

8 eggs

1 cup [200 g] granulated sugar

1 cup [200 g] dark brown sugar

1 Tbsp ground cinnamon

1 Tbsp ground cloves

½ tsp fine sea salt

Whipped cream for serving (optional)

Heat the oven to 350°F [180°C].

Put the piloncillo and water in a saucepan over medium heat, and cook, stirring occasionally, until the sugar is dissolved. Remove from the heat and set aside.

In a large bowl, mix together the torn bread, raisins, peanuts, and coconut. Gently mix in the queso fresco and bananas.

In another large bowl, whisk together the piloncillo syrup, cream, milk, eggs, granulated sugar, brown sugar, cinnamon, cloves, and salt until thoroughly mixed.

Put the torn bread mixture into a deep 9 by 13 in [23 by 33 cm] baking dish. Pour the cream mixture over the bread mixture. Cover with foil and bake for 40 minutes. Remove the foil and bake, uncovered, until the bread pudding is golden brown, an additional 25 minutes.

Serve immediately with whipped cream, if desired. Leftover bread pudding can be stored, covered, in the refrigerator for up to 3 days. Reheat in a 325°F [165°C] oven.

DEDICATION

I wrote this book in honor of the family I grew up with—my great-grandparents, grandparents, uncles, aunts, mom, dad, and brother. And especially in memory of Octavio Rodriguez, Uncle Andy, and Aunt JoAnn.

— JOSEF CENTENO

ACKNOWLEDGMENTS

In the early spring of 1990, I organized a modest rebellion. I was sick of the lunches at my high school cafeteria—frozen food heated in aluminum foil pans and set out on steam tables. So I got a group of other freshman kids to refuse to eat it, and we decided to bring our own brown bag lunches.

As word of our boycott spread, more kids refused to eat what the cafeteria prepared. A local newspaper even wrote an article, quoting several students: "The food's lousy." "We don't want our food to be so greasy." "The cafeteria brings the school down."

The administration wasn't pleased, and someone from the principal's office came up to me in the lunchroom and said, "You have such great parents; it's too bad they have a shit for a son." I told my mom because I thought it was funny, but of course she got involved. Pretty soon, we had a salad bar and meals made from fresh ingredients.

Second high school insurrection: The first semester of sophomore year, I refused to play football. My friend Octavio and I wanted to play lacrosse, but there was no lacrosse team and school officials didn't want one. So along with a band of other misfits (what Texas high schooler doesn't play football?), we joined a club lacrosse league at a nearby U.S. Air Force base. Team Nashua practiced off campus. My dad helped us find coaches, funding, and equipment, and organize weekend games across the state.

Eventually (long after I'd graduated), several lacrosse teams became part of the high school sports curricula in San Antonio. Another local newspaper article honored and quoted my dad: "There is a niche for boys who do not fit into the normal sports system. We have picked up these boys that would have been left out."

This is all to say, THANK YOU, Mom and Dad, for always standing behind me.

Thank you also to the Bar Amá staff, past and present, for all of your hard work. Thank you to Genevieve Hardison, Francisco Flores, Salvador Vasquez, and Fabian Rodriguez.

The authors would also like to thank Sarah Billingsley and Vanessa Dina at Chronicle Books—we're grateful for your beautiful books; the incomparable Kitty Cowles; Ren Fuller for all of her gorgeous photos—and for making that hot, hot trip to San Antonio; Alicia Buszczak for her gracious styling; Jennifer Chong; Deborah Kops; and Kikuko Hallock.

And of course, Bear and Winston.

265

A
M
Á